MY NAME WAS CALLED

Graham Redman

Reading Stones Publishing

Copyright © Graham Redman 2020

ISBN   Paperback: 978-0-6488938-6-8

eBook: 978-0-6488938-7-5

All rights reserved. No part of this book may be reproduced or transmitted in any form or by any means, electronic, or mechanical, including photocopying, recording or by any information storage and retrieval system without the permission in writing by the copyright owner.

Unless otherwise stated Scriptures quoted here are from the King James Version (Authorised version). First published in 1611. Quoted from the KJV Classic Reference Bible, copyright 1983 by the Zondervan Corporation.

Any people depicted in stock imaginary provided by Shutterstock are models and are being used for illustration purposes only

Published by: Reading Stones
                 Helen Brown and Wendy Wood
                 <woodwendy1982.wixsite.com/readingstones>
Cover Design: Wendy Wood

For more copies contact the publisher at:

Glenburnie Homestead
212 Glenburnie Road
ROB ROY NSW 2360
Mobile: 0422 577 663
Email: hbrown19561@gmail.com

Contents

Introduction
1 A life changing event
The bad news
2 Growing up
A major move
3 Teenage development
Friends
4 Being devious
Real romance
5 The early workplace
Military training
Back to the grind
The Beaumont children
6 Country policing
Port Pirie
Mannum
Motorsport
7 That quiet voice
The miracle
… May 1975
A new walk starts
8 Another vice gone!
Alienation
9 Church life
Bible college
The pain of blasphemy
Teacher
Youth With a Mission

10 Missions
China 1988
God in control
The border crossing
India 1999
East Timor 2004
11 Russia
Krasnoyarsk
12 God with us
Camping
Mission trip
13 Moscow
God's presence
Tombov
Koorsk
14 Police resignation
A witness of Bible numerics
The big day
15 The enemy attacks
A private business
16 Another life-changing event
Breakdown
The court case
The shock and the trauma
17 Prison life
Workshop and security demeanours
The parole board
Divine intervention
A light at the end of the tunnel

18 On the way home
Another era starts
Oh no, not again
Another penalty
19 Employment in retirement
The Strzelechi Track
Blue plate taxis
Harley Davidson tours
Now a builder
20 Another trial
A new path
About the Author

Introduction

My Name Was Called

My life started by being raised in the Christian church by my parents with the same background, my father not necessarily a regular church goer that I know of. My mother more so.

This story has been written straight from the heart, showing both the bad and the good aspects of my life experiences, realising that God's graciousness was in control and drew me into His fold by conviction with limited spiritual teaching. The lesson being a matter of choice under that conviction, whereby had I not responded, my life would have been much different resulting in total disaster.

The group of believers in the current era of my life within the fellowship at House of Prayer for All Nations consisted of up to 50 persons, mainly women, married and single, with a minor number of men. It is not a local church open to the public, as they were intercessory prayer warriors, who were involved with spiritual warfare, 24/7 prayer vigils. overseas missionary trips with prayer groups visiting in various countries being the norm. A powerful group indeed, led by Jenny Hagger, an Apostle recognised by many other Christian bodies in Australia and overseas.

Pauline and I now have been with this Ministry for over 11 years, and we have grown together spiritually, especially me exponentially due to the Holy Spirit anointing over the organisation.

Pauline, under Jenny's leadership now is in charge of a library/resource centre of over 10,000 books in the offices at Aldgate in the Adelaide Hills, in the prayer tower in the Adelaide CBD, and also in a motel owned by the fellowship on Kangaroo Island in South Australia.

I must admit that we as human beings have choices, we are not robots, but in retrospect, the choice I made to submit to God's calling was unavoidable. The conviction was so strong that to reject the call was too hard due to the actual trauma of the conviction. I recognised that an answer of a positive choice was the option if my life was to change and be free. I wanted to be free. My teaching backed the decision. For any person who has not had any Christian teaching, any conviction, I believe, would need to be born from personal contact with Christian people evangelically with the conviction coming from the Holy Spirit.

A time of reflection. My wife and I are now aged in our 70's, our three children having left home quite a few years ago now and have given us the privilege of loving our 6 grandchildren. We do not know how many more years we have to enjoy our family, of whom we are very proud, considering that our children are successful in their fields and lead stable lives.

We are a Christian family, all of whom are dedicated to following the example set by our Lord Jesus Christ, in His life over 2000 years ago and His book on the way we should live.

So, this biography of mine is dedicated to setting out my life's challenges to the point now where I feel driven to telling you of the results of these challenges. Therefore, this book is a testimonial, with a religious flavour, pertaining to my life with a thrust to inspire other people in their life choices.

This author, for years, has been wanting to publish in book form, as it is wonderfully comfortable to relax in a chair with feet up and book in hand. My wife of course, Pauline, does this curled up in bed on a nightly basis; she is a librarian, and surrounded by mountains of books.

My publication started many years ago, inspired by a friend's father who wrote his biography for his children and grandchildren to be enjoyed by them as a result of his flamboyant lifestyle so they could perhaps learn about their grandfather through his testimonial.

My life story, I believe, could be of benefit to my children and grandchildren, and hopefully the general public reader, as a testimonial of the results of the huge errors made in my life, perhaps in ignorance, and the corrections made to this past life to improve not only my self-esteem, but to qualify a standard acceptable to other people. Sometimes not so.

I need to add that, in retrospect, I just did not have the conviction required towards being a Christian recognised by my actions. I was a hypocrite. This story therefore includes a change for the better as a result of conviction, whereby faith in God strengthened my resolve.

This story then engages faith as a feature of strength in leading a much better lifestyle, which has created a very positive outlook towards life for me as we all live it, regardless of the horror and pain we experience in this world. It is an intention to publish towards general public reading with a view of helping them in understanding their role in society and drive towards a better life. I had actually written my life story pre the year 2000, but in reading it again after some time, was not at all appealing, as it did not include faith in God, so I scrapped it, but mentally keeping the idea alive.

The drive to publish, ended up sending me on the trail of establishing the Redman family tree, which is historically over 20 years old now in its construction, when computers were basic as was research on the internet. Since then, I have upgraded to an Apple Mac Computer which is now internet based where research results are mountainous, giving far more scope for this book as I could not have envisaged back then. The family history goes back prior to 1000AD/CE

One must understand I may need to change, or refer to first names only, or not mention the names of people, in this dialogue for their protection and anonymity, although very close family and friends I may need to refer to.

I trust now that you will enjoy what the life of yours truly has meant in the learning to live a life of struggle and faith, and may encourage all towards fulfilment.

Why am I putting forward these basic ideas…….?

At my age, 78 at the time of writing, I am becoming more aware of my limitations, so my decision to put pen to paper, or should I say fingers to buttons, is towards understanding my own attitudes and why other people view my personality in ways that they do, which affect their response to me in our relationships and me to them.

I said limitations, but it goes far beyond that, towards failures and mistakes, which have plagued me throughout my life, in some cases, which I will not go into in detail, which change my direction certainly not towards a smooth road, but a very rough one.

As a card-carrying Christian, my witness to other people must include an attitude of loving one's neighbour. This applies to ensuring that the statement above shows no indication of revenge or hate, or any form of adverse comment about that person. It took some years from the offence to actually get rid of any feelings which would cause anger in my spirit to those ends. Forgiveness is the only form of release from those attitudes. It was not easy and would only occur face to face should it be desired. It is a heart thing and I do believe I have settled my heart in forgiving him, and myself over the whole incident.

MY NAME WAS CALLED

Graham Redman

1
A Life Changing Event

This story begins in February 1964, on a particular hot summer Saturday night with my brother Warren, his girlfriend and wife to be, Heather, and Pauline, my wife to be. We had been out together for most of the afternoon and, after having a Burger King meal, went to the Gepps Cross drive-in theatre in my 55 FJ Holden for a movie night. This was a usual routine with us or other friends on any weekend for young people in their early 20s. We had settled down in the car and were enjoying the movie feature, when a notice came on the screen interrupting the movie, reading:

> "Graham Redman, please return home."

A shock went straight to my heart and through my mind as I realised immediately what the problem was, as I saw a picture of Mum lying on her bed that morning in an unusual position which should have rung alarm bells, but it didn't, so we left the drive-in with a conversation starting as to why, but I knew.

My brother was curious, He said sounding alarmed, "It must be pretty serious…"

I said, "Mum's died."

"What! how do you know that?" was the chorus from them in

disbelief.

I then related my concerns of what happened the previous night and what I saw on this Saturday morning but ignored.

I went on, with a feeling of despair, "I saw her in bed this morning in an unusual position and ignored it.... I thought she was just asleep, but now I know."

For quite some time I was aware of tensions between our parents, but was oblivious to what they were. I was aware that our parents were having difficulties for some time even to the point that she wanted to move out and leave our father with us boys. That could not happen in reality as Mum had no income of her own and would have to rely on our income. I still remember the three of us walking down a street to look at another house but being oblivious as to the implications then.

My brother and I slept together in separate beds in the same room of this four-room house, our parents' bedroom in the adjacent room. The lounge and dining rooms being on the opposite side of the central passage of this 1930's cottage.

We were awoken on this Friday night at about 1am by our parents having an argument in their bedroom, and it was so heated that we, my brother and I, went to intervene, instinctively I grabbed a tennis racquet. I did that without thinking about it, with the driver being to protect our mother. When we walked in, she was standing by her bed obviously very distressed and crying. Father was standing by his bed in front of her with fire in his eyes looking quite angry, I noticed his fists were clenched. Our intervention quieted him as I said, "Back off dad, leave her alone...." while I raised the racquet threatening him, I was very frightened as he moved back towards his bed, I didn't know what was going to happen. I then put my arm around Mum's shoulders to comfort her, she was crying and shaking uncontrollably, "Come outside, Mum, please."

We then walked out of the bedroom and I ushered her down the passage, as I cradled her in my arm and held her lightly, being aware at this time that she was suffering broken ribs which had been bandaged. This was apparently as a result of a previous dispute between her and father. We went out the back door and sat on the steps under the Glory vine, weeping many tears together. I was weeping for the first time in my life discovering a compassion I had never experienced, as a love for her built up in my heart. I said to her, "I really love you Mum, I'm sorry I have just never understood. What happened?"

I gave her as much comfort as I could as we talked for a while, telling me about the argument. It all settled down later and everyone retired for the night, both parents together in their room. Warren and I in ours. Mum had assured us that it would be okay before she went to bed.

I tried to sleep, but instead I wept, sobbing as I prayed quietly, something I had never done. I often wonder if Warren did the same, as he must have heard me and my grief.

I prayed, "God help her, God help her please..." over and over until I slept.

I must have had a faith in God down deep which I never recognised, the result of parental guidance in the Christian Church early in life, so this time I used that faith quite unknowingly actually, just out of desperation. My heart was aching for my mother.

In the morning, after a sleep in, as was my brother's and my habit and with the previous night's event dismissed in my mind anyway, we left the house to go meet with the gang/mates for the day, a Saturday. Father was not home, so not seeing our mother as usual in the kitchen and elsewhere, I checked for her in the bedroom and found her still in bed asleep, which was very unusual for her at this time, after 9 am. She was on her back with her arms outside of the neatly arranged covers by her side in a position which did not appear normal. I ignored this even though there was a check in my spirit. I yelled out to my brother saying, "She's alright, she's still asleep, let's go." We then left the house in our cars.

I was more intent of leaving for the day (selfishly) for my pleasure with no more concern for our mother.

So, all this I related to my passengers on the way home from the drive-in.

The Bad News

It is a half hour drive from the drive-in at Gepps Cross to Magill, so the conversation between us dissipated, as I was feeling quite tense and apprehensive. As I drove the FJ left around the corner into our street, my heart started pounding as I was hoping my prediction was not true. My friends in the car with me were quiet as I slowed to steer into the driveway of the house. The rear lights were on, but I could not see anyone at the back door because of the glory vine covering the area between the two rainwater tanks.

I quickly got out of the car, slammed the door and we four together walked up to the back door. We stopped at the stone steps. My father was there with two uniformed Policeman and I suddenly shuddered in the realisation it must be true. Mum had died. So, my concerns were justified.

Father said, showing a face of shock and apprehension, "I'm sorry boys, but your mother has died", His lips quivering as he spoke.

I said, "What happened Dad?" As my heart sank with despair.

He looked very upset, with teary eyes, he paused breathed deeply, and said, "It looks like she took an overdose of sleeping pills. She had been taken by Ambulance to the Adelaide Hospital, but she had died. Her death was confirmed there."

The news was quite devastating! We just looked at each other, my Father, Warren and I, as we three men realised that our lives were going to be different. I can't recall us taking the girl's home.

It was some time before we settled that night, as we sat with father for some time. It was a very sad time in many ways, the worst being that we had lost an excellent mother. At least I had the opportunity to see her that morning, at peace.

Her funeral was about a week later, the Service being held at the Magill Anglican Church on St Bernard's Road. I recall vividly, standing outside the Church feeling very lonely, musing, and as if in an out of body experience seeing myself standing there when I heard a small voice in my mind which said, "It's all right Graham!"

It was that small voice that gave me a confidence that all was well with her death, for a purpose of which I was not aware. I now know that it was Jesus that spoke to me, telling me that she was in his care.

The service was traditional, with the coffin before the alter, covered in flowers, and this time I felt very sad, with some heartfelt emotion, and being teary but peaceful. I can recall nothing of who the people were who gave eulogies, the service, or any other details of the day.

Warren and I, with four other men, then carried our mother from the Church to the hearse. These were the days where the funeral Cortege was a long line of well-wisher's cars following behind the Hearse to the burial place. Mum was cremated at the Centennial Park Cemetery, her remains were to be placed in a memorial wall. The drive was long and slow, but soon over.

Only a few years ago, as a source of respect, the ashes of both parents needed to be recovered from the Park as the term had expired, so Pauline, Warren, Heather, and I went to Mylor near Mum's birthplace and scattered their remains in the Sturt River. It was a tender, yet heartfelt, time for us all to once again to say "Goodbye" to our parents.

Deep grief evaded me; I often wonder why, but now I do consider that I was to suffer that grief for about 12 years. Our mother died at 50 years of age in 1964, in my 23rd year, and Warrens 21st year. I even now miss her terribly, so this is actually quite hard to write about.

I did feel at peace, but tinged with sadness, however, there was one redeeming feature of this incident. This event changed us, I believe for the better, and matured us very quickly. There was an unspoken forgiveness for our father, and a relationship that formed out of necessity, as a result of the event, which we never really had. We became closer with our father and we actually spent a lot of time together, we actually sat down together at night playing cards etc. I still am in awe of the fact that there was no animosity to my father at all that I felt. Is that the nature of forgiveness?

Only a few years later, father met with a woman, whom he had known from his youth, named Sylvia Taylor, a widow. Both were in their 60s and they continued in a friendly relationship, until they decided to marry in 1970. My brother and I were very happy with the arrangement which certainly changed our lives again. Both Warren and I were in the throes of our own married lives with our children growing up, so father sold the Magill property and moved to live with Sylvia at Balaklava. This had me smiling, if not chuckling every time I remember this, as he, living in her house, needed to behave himself and treat her with much respect, contrary to his treatment of our mother. Sylvia even had him attend the local Church frequently.

My brother and I had the opportunity to visit occasionally, until his death in 1977 at age 73. We were told he died peacefully in his sleep, which indicated to me that he may have changed his ways and became a Christian believer, as I understand when I heard God's voice again, saying, "It's OK Graham." Pauline and I continued to visit Sylvia after his death until she passed away only a few years later. It was good that, due to this relationship, we met with her local farming family enjoying their company.

Only a few years ago, being 50 years later, I was reminiscing about my life and the events therein, and being rather teary, suddenly, like a flash of lightning, my eyes were opened and felt a huge pang of guilt and said rather loudly, "I could have saved her…. but I ignored her…… Oh, forgive me Lord…. please forgive me".

This hit me hard. I wept. I realised that had I not been in a hurry to leave the house and enjoy the day with my friends, I could have saved her. My voice continued in repentant prayer to God right away, trembling and realising the difference it would have made in our lives had she lived. It took some time to get over those thoughts before I had a release from that burden, albeit some 45 years later.

Guilt had obviously set in over the years of which I was not aware, but it had affected my life in other ways, mainly in anger and frustration and addiction to tobacco and alcohol; not that I was an alcoholic. Recalling this had me realising that I was grieving over Mum's demise, but not being actually aware of the reason for my mental state. I grieved for 12 years until I met our Lord in 1975.

2

Growing Up

My earliest memories are at the ten-acre property at Aldgate, called 'The Pines', on the Valley Road below the Aldgate School, which my parents bought after moving from our first home at Croydon in the City. I was born in Adelaide in 1941, to parents Clement and Marjorie; Clement being from a large family in Coonawarra in the South East of South Australia on a sheep farm; and Marjorie from a dairy farm at Mylor in the Adelaide Hills. So, they both came from farming families and were self-sufficient. They were married in the Anglican Church at Marryatville, in the south eastern suburbs of Adelaide in 1939. This church was immediately alongside the Marryatville High School, which I attended as a teenager for 4 years. This elated me as it was a surprise at the co-incidence. My Parents then settled in Croydon, quite close to the General Motors Holden factory in Woodville, where Father worked throughout the Second World War as an Aircraft Inspector.

The next 9 years had them move house three times, so I can only assume that tensions were there between my parents, as my father moved us from Croydon to Aldgate Valley only 5kms from Mylor, in about 1943, while I was still an infant so mother could be closer to her family. I understand the reasons, as the maternal grandparents would need to be interactive with Marjorie and me. My father then needed to commute from Aldgate to Woodville by train, a very slow journey through the Adelaide hills. It would have been a considerable sacrifice being away from home 6am to 6pm. This lifestyle could have caused a lot of stress and tension, affecting their relationship. It would have for me under those conditions.

My young brother Warren was born in the Stirling hospital in 1944.

Aldgate was a small village, where personal interactions were negligible, and I started School there. It had only 44 students, housed in a single, four-room, stone building with lean-to offices at its entrance. The building is still there but attached to a new building housing the Aldgate Church of Christ.

To get to the school from the front doorsteps I had to run very fast down a narrow stony path to the road, jumping over a rocky pile of stones where brown snakes were alleged to be present. We named it snake gully. I was always anticipating a brown slither nearby, very frightening.... I was only 6 or 7 years old. Life there was very interesting and fun with many adventures to be had. We had a cow which we milked, chickens which gave us eggs, vegies growing for food, and Father with his shotgun to clear the property of the brown snakes.

A favourite hobby of mine was to climb to the top of a pine tree, one of many, in the back yard, the branches making a ladder worthy of climbing, to be up there with the birds. The branches were staggered so it was easy to climb as they were also close together. The view was the reward, as the house was built above the valley floor and I could see through the other trees and over our back paddock where our cow would graze. There is a medium sized creek that flowed through the front of our property under a bridge just inside our gate. The property was only about one kilometre along the road into the Aldgate township.

Milking time was fun, as father would squirt me in the face with milk from the cow's teat while he milked the cow, a daily occurrence morning and night. A great laugh between us as I opened my mouth to catch the milk. There was a very basic tin shed under the pine trees with a straw strewn floor being the stall for the cow's bed. The milk, a bucket twice a day from Betty, provided us with cream which mum scraped from the top, and the butter which I would watch her make.

One day, Father killed a very long venomous brown snake and he hung it over the side fence with me standing there in my hat and rubber boots, me being the height of the fence and half the length of the snake.... and took a photo which I have for proof.

There were shopping trips with mum into the village where a walk along a very narrow path on the side of the narrow bitumen road was necessary, pushing a pram with my new brother Warren wriggling therein. It was only about 1km from our property to the shopping area, and to a two-storey building, the ground floor being a grocery store. The building is still there but used for a different purpose. It was at the intersection of the Bridgewater Road and opposite the Aldgate Pump Hotel. These were the days when there was a counter between the grocer and us, but with a glass front where I would yell with delight, "Mum, a want a lolly, please buy me a lolly, I want one of them..."

The best memory recollection, of which I was reminded often, was that Father carried me on his shoulders along the shopping precinct as I was yelling 'Choo-Choo' so I was carried to the Aldgate Railway Station in case a train would pass through on its way to or from Adelaide. The village was built on the main highway from Adelaide to places east, and the railway line from the Aldgate Station passes over this main road on an historical stone bridge.

There are other great and wonderful moments of course.

For a child, it was a lonely life on that property as we needed to travel some distance to get to any neighbouring property, whether walking or driving. The Aldgate valley Road was a narrow winding road between Aldgate and Mylor inhabited with other small holding hobby farms and lined with huge gum and pine trees.

The only way people would meet in this local area was through sporting events, football and cricket, along with picnics at the Mylor oval and swimming events at the Silver Lake. So, my interaction with other children was almost non-existent, which I now know could have prevented me from developing essential skills for building friendships in the future and perhaps to develop a confident personality, as I now realise, I lacked. Was this the road to my introversion?

The following events I want to mention, which I believe could have impacted my development.

The family were at a local event at Mylor, playing tennis. It was a fun time for the few kids there, as my brother and I played in the adjacent pine plantation up a slight hill at the rear of the courts. I ran down the hill and nearly sliced open my throat on a fence wire.

That drew the players attention, as they realised, I could have been choking if not slicing my throat open. Thankfully no damage was done. Just an event.

My brother and I playing in the back yard by a rainwater tank and an underground water spring. We were having a fight over some incident between us, so I started belting Warren with a small bike tyre. I was about 5 years old; he was only 3, and he was screaming. We were both in tears, Mum came and intervened, and I was shut in our darkened bedroom for a long time screaming to get out....my punishment which was rather horrific, being in the dark, putting some degree of 'behave or else' respect into me.

In starting school at the Aldgate Primary School, my mother walked me from our property across the Aldgate Valley Rd, up a steep rocky path to the classrooms. She took me to a Teacher in the yard, said goodbye with a hug, and then walked away. I screamed myself to tears crying for mum. I had never been separated from her, never, so I was very fearful of being left alone, I recall vividly the trauma of this event.

Also, at this School, I was usually bullied by a rough and tumble boy, perhaps older than me. He must have seen my weakness in not being able to relate to the other students or to form any friendly relationships as I really did not know anyone, even though there were 44 of them.

After classes finished for the day at another time, this bully chased me across the yard and teased me, so I got up and ran home down this steep rocky path aiming to get home as quick as I could....it happened of course that I tripped over a rock and fell face down breaking my nose. I walked home, blood gushing, crying all the way, to be met by mother at the house. She then took me off to the doctor for stitches in a badly cut nose, suffering more pain when the stitches were inserted. There was a positive here in that I had always suffered with bloody noses during summer; after this incident I never had another one, the fall repaired the problem. The bully never bothered me again.

I believe that the events I just described affected my confidence in my ability to relate to other people. Parental discipline causing trauma, the unknown - perhaps poor relationship - between my parents, the bullying at school, anxiety caused by the loneliness of being left at the school on the first day. In trying to understand myself now, these points tend to be an excuse for my reactions to similar events. I believe it all sounds like a good reason for my behaviour.

I will go one further, as I believe the next incident caused a huge problem in my ability to learn and retain information for which I have suffered all of my life. The next section relates to the move from Aldgate to Magill, 8kms from the Adelaide City Centre.

A Major Move

In March 1948, Father decided to move back to the City, I assume it was due to the tensions of the move from Croydon to Aldgate, so it was back to the City again. They sold the property at Aldgate and moved to Magill in the foothills of Adelaide 5 miles (8km) from the city. The trip from Aldgate to Magill was done at twilight in a 1926 Rugby utility down the very windy highway 1, past the 'Eagle on the

Hill' hotel and petrol station, chug-a-chug with my brother and I jammed in between our parents, and the family cat, of course, trying to jump out, scratching us wildly. It was very uncomfortable.

The house had land which my father wanted, 3 house blocks plus the block the house was built on, a four-room cottage with lean-to kitchen, laundry, and bathroom, and a copper wood-fired water heater, concrete washstand, and wringer. A wood-fired kitchen stove and oven, with electric stove and fridge added later. The front of the cottage had a bullnose corrugated iron and post veranda with a tiled concrete floor. A typical cottage for the era, possibly built in the mid-1930s.

At the time, he was still employed at Holden's factory at Woodville, at Aldgate he needed to travel by steam train from Aldgate to Woodville and back, a 6am to 6pm travel and workday, but in living at Magill it was still a hard day as he was really only home on weekends, so he resigned and then became employed at the Magill wards of the Adelaide Hospital as a Porter. He sold the vehicle and bought a bicycle, so his days were much shorter and enabled him to build the property with fruit trees, a vegetable garden and a large chicken house where he supported 20 chickens for eggs and the occasional chicken meal. Self-sufficiency was still the order of the day.

For me, I started at the Magill Primary School, the original school being in the street opposite our house but facing the Magill Rd. (this School is now an Art gallery and community centre). I was in Grade 3 at this time, and it was only two classrooms, another School having been built on Penfold Rd, one block away to cater for grades 4 to 7.

My Introduction to the school was to be another shock, walking into the classroom I was faced with about 20 other kids my age and an elderly, white haired, small, grumpy, female teacher. This was my first day, not unlike the first day at the Aldgate school, but calmer.

The very first thing she said to me was, "Go and sit in the back row, at the empty desk, there is pen and ink there to be used…do not write on the desk…" as she waved her finger in the air scowling. I did what she asked quickly, trying to avoid the gaze of the other students. She then gave me a sheet of paper, and I was told to fill it in. "Write your name and address on this and hand it back to me."

I had no idea what to do, as I really did not know my full name, and certainly not my home address even though it was across the road. I was only 7 years old, and we had just moved into the house. I said, "But I don't know what to write, I live over there across the street. My name is Graham."

So, I was reprimanded. I was filled with panic, not knowing anyone nor the teacher, my loneliness moved me to silence and lack of any form of self-awareness. I was petrified.

Sometime later, in this class, we were reading a geography book, not bad for grade 3, yes, I could read. Just a page of a printed story with a picture on it. The teacher picked me and asked me a question about what I had read, I had no clue whatsoever, so I was ordered up from my seat and stood in a corner, my memory tells me with a dunce's cap on my head. I was devastated, frightened, and demoralised. Since then, I have never been able to memorise or recall anything I read, I was too afraid of failing to recall what I had read, so I evaded even trying.

Later, in the upper grades, related in the next section, I was being taught the English subject which included poetry. In studying this, I got as far as recalling a few lines of the first verse, but that fear prevented me from attempting to memorise anything further. Contrary to this, in retrospect, my best efforts with English was in spelling, I triumphed at this as the years went on.

What conclusions can we come to at this time. These events, I believe had set a path of severe introversion where I could not relate to my peers, nor have any faith in myself. I do consider that the treatment I received at these crucial times in my development may have set the need for fulfillment, and confidence, among other things.

With our walk through our lives, do we perhaps understand that whatever happens to us, or do we believe our own attitudes and personal drive make our lives comfortable and successful, or do we, psychologically rely on or blame outside influences. In understanding myself and other people who show me their attitudes and personality, it is all in relationships and the need to have those relationships. Affection towards those persons close to us, I believe, can only develop into our acceptance by those around us and us accepting them.

3

Teenage Development

My parents raised me within the Christian Church and its teachings. My father did not show much of his faith, apart from Church attendance at Easter and Christmas, so it was my mother who ensured that my brother and I were entrenched, so to speak, in the Anglican faith in the Church at Magill, to the point that my brother was an altar boy. Our 'religion' was Sunday church attendance and the youth group, but there was no Bible reading or prayer in the family home, and I had never read the Bible. I tagged along with mother and brother to the services and was encouraged to attend the classes for the purpose of 'confirmation' into the church family, which I did. I was confirmed at age 14, and still have that certificate. The part of the services which struck me, and stayed with me, was the Apostles creed, when I read it within the service, I meant it. There was, and possibly still is, a marble plaque attached to the church wall facing the congregation, with these words emblazoned upon it.

"I believe in God, the Father Almighty, Creator of Heaven and earth; and in Jesus Christ, His only Son our Lord, who was conceived by the Holy Spirit, born of the Virgin Mary, suffered under Pontius Pilate, was crucified, died, and was buried."

I often wonder, was this the point of my confession to accepting Christ as Lord? Maybe, maybe not, as there was no repentance, my lifestyle did not change as this story may point out. **That was it really.**

Taking a step back, after my Grade 3 experiences, I moved from there to the Magill Primary Upper Grade School, which was a newer school on Penfold Road, to grade 4, so I started there the next year to be taught by a gracious teacher, Mrs Bennet. (She and her family had a clay pottery business within this Magill area, a few blocks from our home, and is still a successful business there today). The brick school building was elongated with 4 classrooms to Grade 7, a progression to look forward to. I did enjoy my schooling here as the teachers were likeable and the students were generally easy to get along with, not all 120 of them though, as I found bullying was still a trend I had to cope with.

I tried football as a sport there, my parents going to the trouble of buying me the regulation footy boots etc, but my abilities were nil, as all I could do was trot along following the ball around the oval which was adjacent to the school building. I was too afraid of getting hurt in the scrums. My father had been a champion footballer in the south east with the Penola Football Club, so obviously he wanted his son to follow in his footsteps.

I was in trouble again! I was involved in a fight with another boy in the front yard of the School during a lunch break, over what, I have no idea, but I was not the aggressor. Thankfully the male yard teacher intervened, sorted it, and, in one of the best examples of counsel I have even seen, the teacher had us shake hands and apologise. Embarrassment set in as half the School population was standing around us gawking.

This changed my life a degree, a positive outlook and answer to bullying, where Robert, the aggressor, and I became best friends. The first close friend I have ever had. This continued until we were in our 20's and finding our partners. The result of this gave me much confidence and acceptance. It also showed that I could fight back.

These incidences now have shown me a tendency towards being unable to handle confrontation, therefore causing me to avoid it by withdrawing companionship to a degree.

At this Primary School, I soon learnt all about real discipline. In front of the main School building there was a dirt play area, and a very grassy 'paddock' which was behind the grain store on Magill Road. A large group of us students were having grass seed fights by throwing them at each other. My brother got one in his ear. These things creep as if they have legs, so medical attention was necessary to get it out. The result was a line-up of a dozen kids at the headmaster's office, twice through, with that old swipe of the cane which stung fiercely on the palm of the hand, hurt like hell it did. I had never experienced this form of discipline, so I had much apprehension as I edged forward in the line not knowing what to expect, although the howls of the kids from in the office, at least, was a warning.

Time marched on and I completed Primary School with average grades and was signed up for Marryatville Technical High School some 3kms away. This school is still in use, although added to and modified, the thrust of studies now being music.

To describe the School as it was then, a large 2 storey building was situated at the rear of a large football/sports oval, now with a centre 3 storey building and a 2-storey unit on the opposite end to the other. This centre building was being built while I was a student there. An old original stable block of two halves has upper rooms straddling them, containing a café and classroom, and there was a relatively new prefab science and art block opposite. There are two workshop blocks at the rear of the main building for classes in woodwork and metal work, as this was a Technical School for the teaching of trades, which may not be used for trades now. There was also an observatory at the rear, all on about a ten-acre block.

In the first year, the school was in Osmond Terrace, Norwood, for first year students only. This was a totally different situation in which I found myself, as it necessitated riding my bicycle to and from this school which was more like 3.3kms. My apprehension was such that I withdrew into myself, not knowing what to expect, to the point I couldn't really relate to the other students. Looking back, it was a dark time for me. Come lunch time, there was one group of three students who were unruly and kept together, with one hanger on. This group picked on me, obviously at this point in time, being new to high school, and showing a possible weakness, they bullied me. As much as I tried to avoid them.

"Hey, you, Redman, come here, you f***ing runt, gimmee your lunch, or I'll biff you one." The big one said, he looked like he meant it, as he got up off the wooden bench and walked towards me. I was terrified, as he laughed, took my lunch and sat me down with the group. I just sat there and didn't move.

This went on for some time, and this involved a new approach to life in what was out there. They actually cornered me and made it obvious that I was being joined to their lifestyle by coercion. For me, this was a way of preventing the bullying by joining them. So, this group had me on a rope. I assume now that this was another test of my resolve in that big question, "Which path do I take."

There are some events in one's life, I believe, that open up the way to a certain lifestyle as a test of how we handle these situations and our choices. Being with this group, my eyes were opened to pornography, but on a very light scale. Nudist Colony books, really tame, but opened my eyes to the female form. After school, on our bicycles I would travel or walk with that group looking at these books, even in one of their homes. I had never, of course, seen naked bodies before, especially female, so it was always quite educational.

Thankfully, this group never continued into year 9 at Marryatville, so I had no more contact with them, and again, thankfully, I was not involved in their extracurricular activities to any other degree. What it did was to open up my eyes to other aspects of life as, with insight now, I see that they could have been teenage hoodlums/rebels/delinquents, actual people of whom I had no knowledge, or of their style of activity. There was no real media in this era where knowledge of criminals or criminal activity or serious crime was actually known or even published, so I was cocooned to life. I never read newspapers.

At the end of the first year, my route to school changed, being much closer to home, as my bike riding was still necessary but much shorter than going to the Norwood School.

New friendships and associations were made along the way, more so at the 'upper school', some of the boys I knew from the Anglican Church youth group who also attended the school. Generally, my time in high school was mild and I blended well with my peers, but still could not always get on with my own age group but with those slightly younger than me.

I need to mention an incident where I believe showed a tendency to protect myself with violence. I was being pushed around by another boy at the back of the woodwork/metalwork rooms on the back porch. Only because of a build-up in me of a violent streak in the defence of the bullies, who always must have seen an inherent personality weakness in me. I have no idea what he was taunting me about, but I smashed him one and it knocked him back about 6-8 feet (2-3 metres). That was the end of that bully. Suddenly, in retrospect, there was the awareness of me being a one punch man, or a fighter. Not that it stopped the occasional incident. But it indicated a danger. As you read on, you will see the effect this had on my life, leading to my imprisonment for a serious offence.

Friends

At about the time of the transition from primary to secondary school, my friend Robert, who lived in the next block away, was from a farming family in the mid north at Carrmulka, so, when we left school, he got a job as a motor mechanic, and also working on the family farm, so we did not see of each other. My main memory of him was of a joke he played on me. His father was a PMG technician, and so Rob got hold of an old telephone switchboard generator, wired it to the metal door handle on the back door of the house and waited for me to come knocking.

I just grabbed the door handle and screamed as he turned the handle and gave me a 75-volt whack into my arm. It b****y well hurt. We were still friends.

I met up with Ian, at School, a shy boy who was very quiet, who walked awkwardly, but did not appear to be bullied at all. It took a while, in conversation to form a friendship. As I was of similar personality, we seemed to mix easily, and a close friendship formed. He lived about a mile (1.6km) away and so we would visit each other on our bicycles and ride around the area, aimlessly sometimes, but usually to the Morialta Conservation Park in the foothills 5km away.

Ian and I were the same age and went to the Marryatville High School together, but he left at the end of the third year while I continued into fourth year. Ian left School to work with his family Grocery Store at Glenunga. Once he attained his driver's licence he was employed as their delivery man. The business priority was to deliver food orders to households within the local area, which continued for many years with the opening of a second shop near Parkside. Ian stayed with this job until he retired many years later due to his back failing him from carry boxes of groceries.

We spent years of weekend days together travelling around the southern areas of Adelaide during our working careers until I married Pauline but always including him in our lives.

Ian was very frugal, never married, never consumed alcohol nor indulged in any habits detrimental to health. He always bought new vehicles, his first was a Velocete motorcycle. When we would decide to visit the south coast beaches, he would pillion me on the back.

His attitudes changed me as in his company I would match his personality out of respect, and perhaps I may have drawn him out of his 'shell' from my flamboyance. There was one attitude of mine I needed to be careful of but found quite difficult and that was that I tended to lead or control him. To take advantage of. There was the one and only incident of a break in our relationship was when I was out of packet with my finances, and he loaned me some money to see me through. Our friendship soured, and it took a year or more for me to ask what the problem was.

I said, "Ian I can't understand what has happened to our friendship….what's wrong. Have I done something to offend you?" He was embarrassed and seemed to not want to say anything, after a few seconds he said nervously, "Do you remember I loaned you some money last year? You haven't paid me back."

I suddenly realised I hadn't, "Ian I'm sorry, I had totally forgotten about it, no wonder you're upset." He said, "Well I thought you had no intention of paying it back". That hurt. The debt was repaid. I was so embarrassed that something of that nature could destroy our relationship. It took some effort to recover trust between us.

Our friendship continued and is continuing to this day, with the barrier of distance between us as he now lived in Mount Beauty in Victoria, where finally he has a female friend whom he cares for in an informal platonic relationship. Yes, he is still a bachelor.

Wally, with his mother and sister and her 2 children, moved into the corner house a block away from my Magill home in our late teens.

They were Polish and migrated from Poland some years beforehand. Wally and I soon became friends when I introduced myself. The family had been traumatised during the second world war, as Wally's mother, sister and he, as a small child, escaped the German occupation. They slept in chicken houses and lived on whatever they could even old bottles of milk which had fermented. His mother was slowly becoming demented as a result and bought milk which she allowed to ferment to drink it.

Wally and I did mix with other friends in the area, and he attended the Rostrevor College, a Roman Catholic school and its rather large church at Newton. So, our religious lives differed somewhat, me being Anglican.

Our friendship managed to attain a 1929 Model 'B' for sedan which was in good condition but needed work to get it running. We parked it in his back yard, looked at each other, and I said, "What do we do now?" He said, "Haven't a clue Red. Better clean it up I suppose." We were so naïve, that we had no idea, although we did our own work on our cars. That was it, it became a chook house. What a waste.

We were mates but through my lack of wisdom, and naivety, knowing what I now realise, I seriously offended him, and his allegiance to me faded, although I still kept in touch.

When Pauline and I were arranging our wedding in 1965, I asked Wally to be my best man. He had no problem in accepting my request, and our wedding went along smoothly with him being part of it all.

Wally of course had met his match and so He and 'Gidge' wanted to tie the knot, so Wally asked me to be his best man. Now the Catholic Church in my eyes were a 'way out there' religious organisation of huge proportions consisting of mainly Italian people with whom we as Anglicans really did not mix, so yours truly, not understanding the significance, said, "Is the wedding in the Catholic Church down the road?"

"Yes, Red it is. Why?"

"I don't know Wal, I don't think I can. I don't know anything about your Church, it scares me." To be truthful, I was petrified at the thought. So, I told him, "No."

Well, that must have hit him hard, I was really stabbing him in the back. Our friendship dissipated right there, but it did not register in my mind that I had seriously offended him, so I tried to be a friend even after apologising which really did not help.

I did have other friends who lived in the area, through the Church School and sport, so my life through my teens and work life, but too many to mention here. So, life went on.

4

Being Devious

Another aspect of my earlier life, considering I was going through puberty, was the awareness of sexuality. My parents taught me nothing, so it was up to me to find out for myself. In this book I have no intention of going into detail, but to say that I found out easily enough but gently and warily. I did have friends of my age and perhaps younger both male and female where lessons were learnt on how to develop relationships with females of a friendly nature, even though my parents warned me not to have these friendships as I was too young. There were two neighbourhood girls who I spent time with through our mutual age, so they helped in my education by that natural urge of curiosity.

Now, my first real 'girlfriend'. I always rode my bicycle to high school first at Osmond Terrace for that first year, and then at the upper school at Marryatville. I am unsure now when I first noticed her, but I always rode past her house, and occasionally she was outside the house doing something, so I started talking to her. I soon found out that her parents were working, and she was the housekeeper of sorts, so we got to know each other over time. Then I was invited inside as she had work to do in preparing meals for the family. We were both about 12-15 at the time and so, being alone, the friendship grew and we became quite close friends. Needless to say, my education continued. Her parents would not allow me any visits so, after we left school, the relationship faded, and we saw nothing of each other. There was a time much later where we met on the tram on our way home from work, the conversation we had then was our last, even though we wanted to continue our relationship. I could tell that there was a flame there for each other. She then told me they were moving to Perth. So that was it. A great learning curve in life, where relationships are separated by events out of our control; I often wonder what would have developed had the situation been different, would I have married her?

I mention this lightly as, at school, I soon found out about two other types of sexual activity. One is paedophilia, the other homosexuality. These lifestyles I am mentioning, I believe, are presented to us as tests as to our reaction and choices. The first I experienced from my year 9 teacher, a single man who was odd, a music teacher, and who lived with his mother, as I later found. His actions in the classroom and out of the classroom were indicative of his paedophilia, but I do not believe we, as students, were fully aware, but the buzz was of his way of performing discipline. I certainly was not aware as paedophilia was really unknown, once again, due lack of media attention.

His habits, while teaching, were to sit or lean on the front of his desk with hands inside his trouser tops, which may not mean much to many and could have been a harmless habit. Also, if any of the boys misbehaved it was down to the toilets with his cane in hand. He had a go at me once as I suffered from biliousness and I was quite ill one day. He took me into his office and inspected my bare stomach. He did call for a taxi though to have me sent home. This experience made me very wary but indicated that what was whispered in among the students was a good observation of that teacher's activities. So, this was one incident in my life education.

The next learning curve was in years 10 and 11, where two of the boys in my class were obviously good friends but showed there was more to it. Every week we were subjected to sports lessons and participated in interhouse sports days, where, after these events, we were required to shower in the sports room in the old horse stables. It was noticed that their physical attributes and manner of personal traits indicated a different trend. These boys were always close to each other as it was obvious by their habits, and their closeness in the science labs, that there were other areas of male friendship which I now know as homosexuality. There were some other indications also and, to a degree, I was inspired by them. This seemed to be obvious by other boys also. These incidences were, I believe, part of sexual experimentation. I say no more except that these observations always led to other areas, including being involved in reading stories of pornography and the viewing of inappropriate photographs. I thought nothing of these choices as I did not have any idea of the morality involved. My Anglican Church attendance did nothing to indicate otherwise, nor at home where bible reading was not done.

I am hoping that you may understand that my purpose in writing about these experiences is to indicate what social choices I had in determining my future personality traits and moral choices. I was actually affected by what was placed in front of me and made some bad decisions along the way.

I went to finish year 11 with average grades at a time when the Education Department first introduced the Public Examinations in technical schools. The end of school exams were done within the school, where training there was more for apprenticeships than higher learning from high schools [such as the one] where my brother was educated. We, at Marryatville Technical, were given the opportunity to choose which exam system to partake in. I chose not to as, in seeing the exam from the previous year, I felt I may not have been able to pass the subjects.

From here you will see that I moved to a total change in lifestyle. Having left school, I was finding the need to be employed, so I found myself parking my bicycle, that old treadly, and looking to be self-sufficient. Not that I was alert to that ideal, but it appeared to be the thing to do. Finding a job was part of this big change so these two 'things' met. More on that later.

The day came when I turned 16 years of age, with the idea of obtaining my driver's licence. My parents did not have a motor vehicle and most likely did not want me to have one. The licencing was done at the local Police Station. Des Brown was the Sergeant in charge in the station on Magill Road opposite our street next to the institute building. Well, I did study the rule book, for about 5 minutes, and trotted across the road in nervous desperation at this need to be mature - getting off my push bike. I failed. A second try and more study a week later, one had to wait that long, and I passed the test. The licence held proudly in my hand.

The problem now was that I did not have a car. This was another problem which affected my future. My parents had always attempted to have me earn some money and they had actually opened a bank account for me years before, but there was only 50 pounds ($100) in that account. At this stage, in early 1958, after leaving School, I met up with a couple of 'friends', one of whom had a 1936 Morris 840 tourer that he wanted to sell for 50 pounds. We drove it around a local horse trotting track and to me, who knew nothing about cars, appeared to be a good vehicle. Against my parent's advice, I bought it. My first car! It turned out to be a bomb, blowing great clouds of smoke from the exhaust which obliterated any chance of being able to see anything behind the car. It wasn't long in my learning experience that I drove it into a deep creek trench, destroying it. I sold it to a wrecker for 25 pounds. So, this started my road to ruin in buying cars by putting me in debt. Then I bought a 1948 Morris 8 tourer which I wrecked, then came my best buy, a 1955 FJ Holden sedan, in which I courted my Pauline, teaching her to drive, which I am sure increased my blood pressure problems. We, along with other friends, would go to a drive-in theatre, or to a dance somewhere, even to coffee lounges in Hindley Street in our free time, enjoying life to the full without a care in the world.

Real Romance

During my time of employment, and being a late teenage hoon, weekend boozer, and self-trained mad driver, I soon realised that, even after having several lovely young ladies to flirt with, I knew nothing about how to have serious relationships with them. A huge learning curve blessed with huge respect for the ladies but with quite short-term affairs. It must have been my bad breath and lack of deodorant. I mean, I only bathed once a week.

That is until I met Pauline. The Wonderland Ballroom at Mitcham, a well-known large meeting of dancing enthusiasts, which, in that era, was a hugely popular pastime on Saturday nights, and at other large venues, like the Norwood Ballroom, as well. The perfect place to meet and pursue young ladies in courtship. About 500 young people were there, boys on one side of the room and girls on the other, so when each dance was called, there was a rush of mingling as our partners were sought.

The dance had been going for about 30 minutes after Alan and I had arrived, and we had been dancing with a few different young ladies enjoying the night. I was sitting out one particular dance when I saw this very attractive, slim brunette sitting by herself on the other side of the room. 'Here goes' I said, and I walked across and asked her to dance. Pauline by name, she turned out to be a perfect dance partner. We blended together, moving as one, she followed easily flowing with the 'Modern Waltz' with modern music from the band on the stage. Together we moved around the floor in the 'Two Step', 'Three Step' and other popular dances, moving in unison holding each other close. We never stopped dancing together on this night. Our conversation was interesting as we seemed to just click and did not stop being together. We found that we both lived in the same area, me at Magill and Pauline at Payneham. Alan matched with his dance partner who also lived in a similar area, and so, we convinced our girls that we should stick together for the night.

At the end of the evening, Alan and I both took our new female friends to their respective homes. We were travelling in Alan's car, so Pauline and I took the back seat, enjoying each other's company. We never let go of each other, cuddling and kissing as we travelled. I said goodnight to her at her house and Alan then took me home. I walked Pauline to the back door of this 1930's bungalow not wanting to part, but Alan was waiting.

"Can I please see you again?", I said nervously holding her tight.

She just looked at me, eye to eye as we were, and nodded, "Yes, if you want to."

"I do, can I see you next weekend?"

"Yes OK", she said softly, so I kissed her.

I left her at the door, and as I walked down the driveway, I puffed and drew a deep breath, my heart pumping, "Wow", I whispered to myself with a big grin, I had something to tell Alan that night.

We continued to meet together often, as I found her to be a great companion. I quickly met her family, Norm and Nancy, in the next few weeks, and found that they were a dedicated Uniting Church family, with her sister Heather, and brother Jeff. It did not take long before I started going to Church with her and we continued dating until we were married in December 1965. Now, after 54 years, we are still great friends and partners, living debt free, thanks to Pauline and her budgeting skills, and have three great children, now adults with their own wives and children.

Pauline was pregnant when we were married, and then, the need for accommodation brought about the decision to move to a country posting in the Police Department as mentioned elsewhere in this story.

The wedding, a budget affair with the Church service commitments to each other, a luxury Dodge limo, where the Bride was driven from her house to the Church 100m away, and then we were driven around the block and back to the church hall for the reception. Oh Boy! Yours truly a nervous mess, it was important for us grooms to make a speech, and I muffed it, I had no idea, it was very embarrassing.

On our honeymoon, we drove to Albury in New South Wales in our old English 55 Wolesley special sedan, and then to the top of Mount Kosciusko, where I was wanting to spoil Pauline with a meal in the Chalet there. My first taste of her budgeting skills was made known very well, as we had our very first 'discussion' right there, where we had to make do with a sandwich. I knew immediately who was to arrange our income. The trip to the top was worth the visit anyway, in an area devoid of greenery, a very rocky mountain, with solid ice on the ground in the shadows below the summit.

Our son Adrian was born within weeks of settling in Port Pirie, a solid baby who taught us quite a few lessons as we raised him, with help from the neighbours and other people from the local church once we were settled in.

I am still learning of Pauline's character and strengths, as life together has been rough at times, as my personality tended to be loud and controlling, which, as time went on, added to my frustrations and, at times, angry outbursts. There were many incidents in my life which showed an edge of lack of control which tended to affect our relationship, money being the main one. My hobbies, the main cost being the sports buggy, which did strain our budget. Once this car was disposed of, it changed to model railways, but, by this time, I managed to live on a weekly allowance to that end.

Pauline, I know now, is showing her true strengths in forgiveness, acceptance, and a love for me which knows no bounds, as a result I have buckled under with the object of loving her back which is my job according to Godly principles. The reader may understand that the trauma of my life which brought about my emotional failures and detention have proven what a dedicated wife she is. I was settling into a more acceptable lifestyle with Pauline, who was a real influence in loving me and accepting me for the lout that I really was. To this day, I still do not understand, what Pauline saw in me, nor her parents, as I must have come across in a poor light, knowing what I was like, a smoker of camel ciggies and a lover of portagaf beer and southern comfort whiskey, a foul-mouthed young man, who had no idea how to manage his finances, being always in debt. Not a good combination, especially when I drove a Morris 850 car. I almost retched when I sat in the driver's seat in the mornings from the ciggy smell in the confined space in the vehicle. But Pauline loved me, always holding me close, showing she actually needed me as much as I needed her. Our relationship is improving every day. This will be shown in the events in the following Chapters.

5

The Early Workplace

My adventures into employment, on leaving High School, had me thinking; where does a man look to his future financial capabilities? There was no guidance from the school for the student to move into a work environment suited for his school achievements. I knew I was good at the subject of 'Building Drawing', but no direction was offered to start with a Drafting job.

My first employment was at the end of the school year, suggested by a relative, working at the David Jones Department Store in Rundle St, Adelaide - the premier shopping district. It was for the Christmas shopping rush. I applied for the job in sales in men's ware, and was given 5 minutes training to sell ties, socks, and stuff. I had absolutely no idea and wrote out dockets for all the items sold. My supervisor, after a complaint, said to me, "Have you not heard of a cash register?" Oops.

There was one very positive and exciting event which occurred at David Jones. I met Dawn Fraser, who was employed there, as she was ushered off in her Olympic uniform from the store at the end of the day, for the 1956 Olympic Games. I shook her hand and said, "Good on you, muscles". I hope she wasn't offended.

The year 1958 saw me fully enter the workforce. My old friend

Robert suggested I speak to his father who was a technician in the Franklin St Telephone Exchange. As a result, I applied for and got the job of 'Technician in Training', a 5-year course with the Post Master General's Department.

My first day, 8.30am, saw me waiting at the front door of the P.M.G. building in Pirie St with other young men, teenagers, waiting to enter the building. Once the doors opened, we were shown into a large workshop area. A day of introduction to the course showed us a classroom and a large practical workshop area with an open wall in the centre, used for phone installation lessons. The classroom for the electronic lessons.

I enjoyed the practicalities of the course dealing with installations of equipment but had no understanding of the electronics needed in applying that knowledge to the construction of circuit diagrams. Here also was the means of working with perfect strangers and forming relationships. Time went on as we got to know each other, under the supervision of our instructor, so as I kept very quiet, I slipped back into my shell which brought out the old problem.

Here is another reminder of my future attitudes as there was one student in the school who was a bully and was always belting me with a steel ruler. He lived to regret it when I fought him to the floor, sat on him and pummelled his head. I was becoming a violent person as being an answer to my introversion. Now after 50 years we meet every year at a reunion as friends.

Here was a problem for me, as, after 3 years, I had no idea regarding electronics for what they were, no understanding at all, and after failing my year 3 exams, I was moved out into the practical field of subscriber telephone exchange installation and maintenance. The one most important lesson here was basic wiring work, which saw me excelling in much later years with my hobby of model railroading in wiring techniques. In my fifth year, in a job I enjoyed, I reported back to Roberts father, who then suggested I get out, as there was no future there for me. The wages were poor as well. So much for his advice in the first instant.

An incident occurred during my early years of employment, at a time when I was driving around, doing nothing, with mates in my then Holden FJ sedan car, when, for some unknown reason we ended up being harassed and chased by a carload of bullies trying to run me off the road. I drove around the suburbs like an idiot, attempting to put distance between us. They eventually gave up, probably because of my superior driving ability!! We call the attitude of the occupants of the other car now, 'Road Rage.'

This event gave me the incentive to counter these problems, and for the wrong reason. I was accepted into the Police Department in August 1963 for police training in a 17-week course, held at the Police Barracks at Thebarton, for mature age trainees. I was 22 years old at this time. We studied law subjects in the classroom, with practical exercises to assess ones' capabilities. My failing was self-confidence, as you may imagine me trying to address 20 other trainees in public; possibly not, I was petrified, but got through it. The other trainees gave me a 'pass' out of sympathy. I had never faced this before with adults, apart from my wedding, but you may recall my Grade 3 experience where any confidence disappeared. A realisation came to me that, in my interactions with about 30 other people within this training, this was the first time that I was never bullied or put down. I must say that this training got me over my inferiority and introversion, coupled with the Government authority powers in Law. There were two main aspects of this training; the military discipline designed for parade drill in marching etc, and then the driver training where our driving skills were enhanced beyond the general public expectations. One other aspect, which was a total waste of time, was the physical fitness regime, running from the Barracks to the Zoo and back along the Torrens River, about 5kms. I had never run much at all since school, so it was very hard for me. Since training ended, I never ran even a mile throughout my career.

I finished the course successfully and commenced active duty in January 1964 on mobile patrol and foot duty in the City and suburbs. The supply of uniforms, a baton, Police Cap and a .38mm automatic pistol, and my Police number 1536, were the weapons of warfare in the sworn duty to protect the public, and to clear the streets of the criminal element to the best of our ability.

Military Training

One other part of High School life led me into the area of the Military training into the future. In the 1950's compulsory National Service continued after the Second World War, where on attaining the age of 18 years, there was the requirement to serve 2 years in the Armed Forces. While at the Marryatville High School there was a brigade of Air Force Cadets, the 'A.T.C', run by one of the Teachers. I joined this brigade and spent year 11 in Military training. It was the whole bit with uniforms, drill training, a camp, and lectures at the North Adelaide training centre, where we learnt aircraft identification and other necessities.

Once I left School, I continued with another year through the North Adelaide base, while becoming less interested due to the complexities of Airforce training and flying. My memory problem showed up here where I could not memorise any aircraft types or any other required details, so any future here was not viable. I understand now that other high schools also had Airforce Cadet Units, obviously as recruitment drives into the Airforce.

Once being employed in the Postmaster General's Department as a trainee technician, and then turning 18, I was actually called up for the National 2 years compulsory military service, but due to this P.M.G. employment being an essential service, my application was deferred on the condition of signing up for Citizen's Military Service, C.M.F, which I did. During that year of 1959, I was conscripted, part time, to do Basic Training and attached to 10 Coy R.S.A.R. Torrens Parade Ground, and then transferred to Hampstead Barracks, which was 8 Company Transport. It was there that I stayed until my transfer to Port Pirie in the Police Department in 1966, where I continued with my Army Service attaining the rank of Lance Corporal.

8 Company was a dream job, although hard work at times, where I was trained, and drove the English Land Rover 4wd general purpose vehicle, and the American International CL transport truck for troop transport and general stores. The depot stored about 4 Landrovers and 10 trucks, with a regiment of about 30 personnel. The organisation here was part of a yearly 14-day camp based at Cultana near Whyalla, and 4 weekends throughout the year. War games was

the order of the day, with the C.M.F. within these camps, so the comradeship in the Units was unique, and friendly, but overshadowed by the Commissioned members authority. This was good for me and settled me into these routines, but also did not help with my self-confidence.

There were just a couple of incidents here worth mentioning, to make life interesting, apart from what may be included elsewhere. On one camp, the Unit was required to transport explosives from the Gladstone storage in the Flinders Ranges south of Port Augusta, to the Cultana Camp, a distance of 123 miles (200km). I often wonder, in hindsight, which would be safer, to drive at the maximum speed of 50mph (80kph), carrying the explosives, or do what the Army required and travel at 20mph (32kph). The other requirement is to travel in convoy 200 yards apart (630m), and to stop and rest on the hour. It took 6.5 hours, at that 20mph speed. Please note this trip was pre 1966 and pre decimal changeover from imperial. It took 3 hours to drive to Gladstone then load up with the explosives which were to be used for live ammo weapons training for the several hundreds of personnel in the Cultana area.

The drive at the required speed led by our NCO in a Landrover, was very hard. Heavy eyes trying to close led to eliminating the drone of the engine by changing gears from 4th to 3rd and back continually, as with the sunglasses, on the head, off the head. No radios to temper that consistency, I could talk to my co-driver if I had one. Oh, and by operating the accelerator on and off, as the convoy of up to 10 trucks concertinaed back and forth. A trip one would not want to do often.

On another trip, which was local at Cultana, was from the camp to the beach in the Spencer Gulf and back, where a constant shuttle of shell grit was needed to bed the dust tracks into roads, as the dust was brown powder which was the destroyer of polished boots. The track to the beach was steep, easy enough going down, but not so much going up with a load of 3 to 4 ton of shell grit. Apart from troops and stores, I had never carried a load of that weight. The International has a 4-speed gearbox synchromesh gears 2nd, 3^{rd,} and 4th but a long draft change to 1st a crash change, and with a 265 c/i engine. I mention this to indicate my fears driving up that hill of about 400meters to the top.

My fears were soon realised when I drove from the beach on a flat section where I changed from 1st to 2nd gear, at least I had some confidence to tackle the hill. Soon the rrrrr....rrrr of the engine started to die.

"Oh s#*t, bloody hell," I yelled as I feared it would stall, so I stabbed the clutch down, grabbed the lever, floored the accelerator, then rammed the gear lever the full 3 feet, almost through the dashboard, into first, dropped the clutch, and kept my accelerator on the floor.

"Go girl, go", as the higher pitched rrrr.... rrrr.... rrrr, of the engine pulled the whole truck and its load jerking under an extreme struggle to gain height.

My hands and knees were shaking, and the sweat was soaking my shirt, through my fear as we climbed the bloody hill. This was very real, and I would never want to experience that dilemma again. The best thing was it taught me how to double clutch.

Two other experiences taught me about truck stability.

The first was at a weekend camp. It was at a site near the beach of the Gulf between Port Pirie and Port Augusta, where I was driving the stores truck, on a track to the site off the main Highway 1, in a convoy of mixed vehicles. We needed to negotiate a small creek about 6m wide with low but steep banks, water worn. I needed to stop to allow the previous truck to cross over, so I noted the course he took, and so I did the same, but my load caused the rear of the truck to buck sideways as the rear negotiated the bank. It got through fine and to me, easy, but on stopping at the campsite, my mate Davey, driving the truck behind me said, "Hey Graham, did you know you nearly tipped the truck over going through the creek?"

I said, "No, it bucked a bit, that's all."

This incident made me realise that the truck cab and the rear cargo bin, sitting on the chassis, twist separately when negotiating rough tracks, as the chassis is flexible.

The second was a trip from the Tailem Bend army shooting range back to Adelaide after a day of firearm training, several trucks were carrying troops, jam packed of course, standing room only. Then came the drive down the winding section of the road from Crafers to the Big Gum tree. I knew that the troops would be having trouble, so, along with the other trucks, we were travelling at a minimum speed, about running pace, because of the camber on the bends - good chassis twisters. There was a lot of noise coming from the troops and I heard someone yell, "Hey slow down, will ya...".

"OK, trying...." I yelled.

When we all arrived at Hampstead Barracks, I jumped from the truck cab, and went to the rear, and dropped the tailgate to let the troops out. One soldier jumped down and yelled, "Where's that bloody driver, I'll kill him, we could hardly hang on coming down Mt Barker Rd, he was going too fast...."

I said, (being the driver,) "OK I'll tell 'im."

That's my Army.....

It came to the time when I needed to tell my C.O. at Hampstead about my transfer to Port Pirie in the Police Dept. He was not happy, as I saw his eyes showing anger when I told of the transfer.

"Sir, I need to tell you that I am being transferred to the Port Pirie Police."

He said, throwing his pen at the desk, "Mr Redman, this changes things, I was going to upgrade your rank and task as a driving Instructor, as your work here is exemplary. I wanted you to stay here, I am very disappointed."

That was a blow. I would have loved that job, I was embarrassed, facing him at the 'At Ease' position. He was then left with no alternative but to transfer my Army station to the depot at Port Pirie. This was a blessing actually, as my service continued as driver/storeman when I transferred. This was the best time I ever had in the C.M.F. as I worked with a gentleman WO2 regular Army man and gained much experience and perks as his right-hand man.

There were challenges in the Army, but as a driver/storeman there were privileges. Food and liquor flowed freely, as did gambling, and the occasional flirt with female soldiers, but try as one did, they were more interested in male soldiers with rank. When serving at Cultana, near Whyalla, on the yearly two-week camps, I recall vividly the free Saturday nights, beer cans being dropped empty, and porn movies displayed for all to see. I had never seen movies like this before. So, in painting a picture of the Army culture at these camps, it was obvious that morality disappeared quickly, which did affect my attitudes and moral drive, another lesson in my education of life in the world. What I refer to is the poor relationships and attitudes of some WO2's to the troops, which I experienced firsthand, by being persecuted and treated like a number.

Once we moved back to Adelaide, I was transferred to R.A.E.M.E, the engineering section at Warradale, due to my interest in motor mechanics, as I did all of my own car repairs and servicing. When I applied for the transfer, I was offered to be transport NCO for the Medical Corp, which I rejected; this was a mistake, as it would have been a cushy job. As a result, I was not looked after in the Engineers, as, when on camps, I was treated like a leper and given severe tasks and no consideration. This was born home when, at a camp, a team of us were taken for a trial lesson in a tracked troop carrier. All of the men except me were trained. I subsequently resigned from the Engineers, as it was obvious the WO2's in charge hated Police personnel, and I was still a serving member. I had enough of bullying. That was the end of my Military career in the C.M.F.

Back to the Grind

Life in the Police Department settled me; various duties; like walking the city streets on beat duty, minor traffic control, and mobile patrol work had its rewards. The uniform certainly gave that authority I was looking for, where, if members of the public infringed, then they had to buckle under and accept the penalty, which in some cases was hard to administer for minor offences, but the rewards for more serious offences was worth the effort. Court duties also were rostered, so much was learnt there for the who's who book. This authority was boosting my confidence, which I certainly needed.

In this era, the Police building was in Angas St, on the southern side of Victoria Square, alongside the Magistrates Court building on the corner of King William St. Our particular shift team of about twenty men, in our black/navy blue uniforms, were paraded in a tin shed at the rear of the Police building alongside the Police cells which were behind the court rooms. Our tools of trade were a baton stored in a pouch in our right trouser leg, a browning .38 pistol clipped on a 'holster' in our right pocket, and an ancient clackety-clack typewriter for our reports. Actually, I still have my black trouser belt which I can just still wear - just. Another boost to my confidence.

Another nail in my emotional coffin very early in the first year, was with the use of that .38 pistol which we were issued with. Yes, we were trained to use it in a pistol range to be licenced within the Department. This experience, even though minor, tended towards indifference to life. For example, dogs which may have been hit by cars or having attacked other dogs or persons, in that era, when on duty, we were required to kill/destroy them. It still took courage to point the gun to the dog's head and pull the trigger. My mind could not think about it, an immediate decision had to be made, no hesitation. In one way, my Army training in firearms use made the use of the pistol easy, but to actually destroy a life was much harder.

I spent only one year on general patrols in the City, which was quite an experience. The City was divided up for 3 patrol cars, one car for the north west corner, one for the north east corner, and a cage car, for prisoners, on the south side of the CBD. The suburbs were divided into 4 areas, north south east and west. These recollections are almost hilarious when I consider the small Adelaide population and, by comparison small traffic flows, hence the works loads were light. A very different story now. Experience was gained in court duties, giving evidence for prosecution cases of my reports or arrests of serious offenders, attending serious accidents, drunk drivers, domestic violence, street fights, deceased persons, and other offences which are the daily duties of Police members.

Then there was a call for volunteers to start a motorcycle course to increase the fleet of traffic motorcycles. Having motorcycle experience under my belt, I applied for that course, and found my experience sadly lacking. We were riding a fleet of 1950's English BSA 650cc street machines. And the one place I never thought the instructors would take us was to the Tennyson sand hills. Riding in sand on a street machine was not funny, our instructor broke his leg when his foot slipped off the foot peg in front of it and 'snap'. At the same time, I went over the handlebars trying to navigate between two dunes.

This era was one of the best experiences in the Police Department as a motorcycle traffic cop. To be paid a wage for what was a dream ride around city streets.

I passed the practical course and was then identified as a 'Speed Cop'. As a result, motorcycle patrols around the City were experienced successfully, where I, as an example, was rostered to patrol Anzac Highway. We were all given a particular main road to patrol for the day.

The Beaumont Children

I also joined the Emergency Operations Group, now known as the SAS Star Force, a heavily armed task force specifically highly trained 'Army'. Unfortunately, it did not last long as I appeared to be unable to get a leg in, so to speak. But I was able to be included in one notable event in the history of South Australia. That is the disappearance of the 3 Beaumont children.

We were living at Aldgate at this time, and I had finished my afternoon shift at 11pm, ridden home, and retired for the night, when I was awoken at 1am, and ordered to the Barracks for duty. A major search had been organised in the Department, and we traffic Police were allocated tasks for search. One of my team and I were allocated a dream job, albeit difficult, but required. We attended at a residence in Colley Tce, Glenelg, to be introduced to a senior member of the Port Adelaide Yacht Club. We then were driven in his Bentley saloon car to the Yacht Club at Port Adelaide, to board his 35' yacht. The task was to search the coast from Outer Harbour to Marino and return to search for the possibility that the 3 children had been drowned. This we did, which took all day in good weather with a rippled sea, and in good company. Our search proved fruitless, with our return to the barracks and then home again after 6 hours on the water. In those two days from about 8am to 6pm the next day, it was 34 hrs with 2 ½ hrs sleep. Them's the breaks.

I am reminded of another job tasked at Easter time in 1964, a good start to a career, with a missing patient from the Northfield Mental Institution. This Easter day recorded temperatures of 40 degrees C and over. The man was reported missing on the Thursday, and his remains were found at the rear of houses on Fosters Road lying face down. My first 'rotten' deal. I will save you from the details, apart from the fact that the Ambulance conveyed the body in a metal coffin in a trailer behind the vehicle, of which we caught the drift. Pauline could detect a strange smell about me when I got home after that shift.

As I mentioned earlier, Pauline and I were married in December 1965, after she discovered she was expecting our first child. So that changed things somewhat. For us, especially me being still quite immature really, I had no idea how to plan our future. The one thing we did do was to purchase a block of land in the southern suburbs of Adelaide. Her family were devastated, as any mother of a teenage daughter knows, when their lessons tend to be ignored. The grief, for them deeper as a Christian family devoted to God. My father, now living by himself was not keen to have us living in the house with him, so we only stayed there for 3 months before moving to Aldgate to live in the house with my late mother's sister. This meant that we needed a house and what with no thought of how this should be when we were married, we entered into the vows in ignorance but then the call of parenthood and the necessity of somewhere to live was a loud call. But then the Department had worked that out, as a Country Posting came with a house for cheap rent. Port Pirie was the town we were heading for.

6

Country Policing

Port Pirie

The transfer to Port Pirie was interesting, in that having been living on the Market Garden at Aldgate, the Department are obliged to take care of moving the goods of the transferee to the new posting. A furniture van in the form of an articulated truck arrived, but got stuck on the steep gravel driveway, so a tow truck was needed to tow the truck to the top of the driveway. Very embarrassing as we had virtually no furniture.

The City of Port Pirie is located on salt flats, as is most of the City, which can be prone to flooding. The City supports a large lead smelter industry and a port which is used for, not only the export of lead products, but wheat and other grains grown in the area. There are about 30 silos used for the receipt and storage of the grain.

The railway yards are historically very important not only for the Port, but as a transitory yard for goods due to the two gauges of narrow- and broad-gauge rail joining here, and also for rail shipping of grain prior to the silo's being erected.

Similarly, for passenger train transport between Adelaide Port

Augusta and Alice Springs, local and Interstate. It is also famous for the longest platform in the State at 1km.

The area of housing where we lived was in Evans St just off Three Chain Road, south east of the CBD. The house there was a brick Housing Trust property among several other houses also occupied by other Police staff, and Patrol men.

Pauline was heavily pregnant with our son Adrian, when we moved to Port Pirie, so she needed our car, a 1955 Wolseley sedan, so yours truly was relegated to riding a 1948 New Hudson auto cycle to work.

This 'bike' was given to me by Pauline's father who used to for transport prior to him buying his first car many years before.

So, with me riding it to work must have turned heads, seeing a uniformed Policeman riding this tiny, motorised bicycle the 2 km's to work and back. I cannot help but laugh at myself every time I think about this. My second effort at being a motorcycle cop.

The Police Station was a two-storey brick office building on a large block situated on Mary Elie St, the main thorough fare. It faces the wharf opposite where the wheat silos are and alongside the Railway Yards. Lines from the rail yards cross Mary Elie St here to service the Lead Smelter and the Silo's.

It was manned by 20 patrolmen, officers and other staff. A 24-hour patrol district of two uniform patrol vehicles and also a C.I.B. Division. Night shift was always quiet, so patrols cruised with few tasks if any, and were made through the Lead Smelter Plant area, wharves, and huge railway yards as well as the residential areas.

Depending on staff some nights were one-man patrols. Much was learnt at this station, on Country Policing and all manner of nice and nasty jobs. While stationed at Pt Pirie I became eligible to study for and sit for the first-class constables' exams which would earn me a First-Class Constable stripe. This occurred after four years' service, so that put me in a position of senior man in any two-man patrol with a Constable. Then after my 10th year I gained a two stripe Senior Constable position. This did not happen until Pauline and I moved back to the City in 1972.

Generally, my work there was rewarded in some ways. One of my workmates Trevor and I were tasked to investigate a missing person. The report came from the Pirie West Hotel where the man was last seen. This Hotel was built on the salt flats along with the suburb of Port Pire West among saltbush fields. I spoke with the Publican.

"So, what happened here Bob?" He was upset to the point of showing some emotion as he told the story.

"My barman was cleaning up and went out the back with the garbage near the sewer drainage trench, and there was a hat floating in the water, which looks like old Fred's. He is a regular here and, on his way, home he walks across the flats at the back. We haven't seen him for 2 weeks so we are worried about him. We think he fell in the trench." I responded looking at Trevor and said,

"We had better have a look then." "OK mate," as he stared back at me Glumly.

We looked alright, Trevor lifted the hat and sure enough, we saw what we didn't want to see. There was a human head under it. If this was Fred he must have died and fallen into sewer drain. It was a 'rotten' deal and my second experience of finds of this nature. Trevor and I were required to recover this body, and investigate the circumstances, which also required identification by the Publican and submit a report for the Coroner for the cause of death. We were commended by the Station Commander for the investigation as to the circumstances in the compilation of the Coroner's Report.

These events for any Police Member and including myself, are traumatic and they do have an effect on your ability to show compassion, if at all. This over the years did affect me considerably. The list goes on, as in Country postings Police must attend fatal road accidents in all areas. I could tell you many stories. This continued when we transferred to Mannum in 1969.

I will mention two events. Our local Doctor at Port Pirie was also the pathologist, and so as I was working a day shift, I was allocated the job of assisting him in a post-mortem, I was to take notes as dictated on that PM. I was shocked when I realised it was for a deceased 18-month-old baby. I felt rather pale as Pauline and I were new parents at that time. The Doctor was very good and told me not to consider the deceased as a baby, but, as hard as it sounds, he told me to treat it as an animal carcass. That did make a difference but being present was still tough. The Doctor showed me a tiny heart in the palm of his hand showing that the child died from a calcified heart valve.

The second was another post-mortem on a 12-year-old boy. This child was on the Adelaide train going to Port Pirie at the Coonamia railway Crossing where the train moved onto a siding. The boy leaned out between the concertinas between the carriages and his neck was broken as the train straightened. This one was quite hard, yes, but easier than the last.

Another incident which could have had severe consequences, but not necessarily for me, was on another job at Port Pirie when a violent incident happened on a property at a BBQ gathering of friends. A young man was killed in the incident, and when I came on duty that night, I was tasked to guard the scene for the night as it was considered a homicide. I was not to interfere with anything at the scene, but then the meat on the barbie was tempting and tasty. The consequences came when I was on leave in Adelaide and the Court case of the murder charge was being heard. So, out of interest as the guard, but not being a witness who needed to be called, I attended at the Court as a learning experience in the results of the hearing. The twist in this case was that I was acquainted with two people involved who were at the original party. And I spoke to both of them in the Court hall.

Big mistake. I was spoken to by one of the Detectives and asked to leave the Court, as the two I spoke to were witnesses in the case, of which I did not know, one for the prosecution and the other for the defence.

This was a serious breach of decorum, which could have caused a re-trial, of course I had no idea of the situation with the witnesses, so the sausages were a bitter taste of experience.

At the end of the term stationed at Port Pirie, I applied for the

Mannum 3-man Station and moved there with our Adrian, 3 years of age.

Mannum

Mannum Station, which was opposite the River Murray Ferry, was manned by a Sergeant and a Constable, and so I joined the team as the second in charge, as a first-class constable. My time there was not good, as the Sergeant was dictatorial, ready for retirement, and hard to work with. Kevin, the constable was serious minded, but we worked well together, but were not friends.

Pauline and I were given a Police House away from the Station, and settled in. The house was timber construction on a large corner block, having a moderate veggie patch, a garage and paved area at the rear of the house.

Kevin and I did most of the work together being my junior partner for the 3 years I was there, but eventually through a serious mistake or two, caused by me, he stabbed me in the back resulting in my transfer back to the City. The only relief I had there within the workload was when the Sgt was on leave, and I was the relief 'Sgt', but when Kevin was on leave, I was just the lackey doing what the Sgt wanted.

I am loath to mention the cause of this next incident, but Kevin and I started a car club so as to be involved in the Adelaide Hills Car Clubs in competition. I had been building the old Vanguard vehicle as I have mentioned, which I designed for road use actually, but that did not happen so that was one reason for the car club so I could drive it off road. Like an idiot, I had actually completed the build and needed to get the car to the main street garage for some reason, and I drove the car there and back home. It was not only unregistered and not insured, but I should not have driven it. So, I showed the locals a hypercritical Police Member committing a very serious driving offence.

On a lighter note, the best part of the job here, was the nature of the work where all events, whatever, which needed Police intervention were attended to. Local Court debt summonses, fatal motor vehicle collisions, suicides, domestics, learner driver testing, Court work, and many other works. This general work I always enjoyed.

Driver Testing, River road, following south along the River Murray, ended in a steep hill up and over the riverbank. I loved this as a perfect test for a handbrake start in a manual vehicle for a learner. I had the driver stop halfway up the hill, and then I asked that driver for their wristwatch. I got out of the car put the watch in my pocket, got back in the car to tell the driver their watch was on the road in front of the left rear wheel. No driver ever failed this test.

I must give credit where credit was due with Sergeant Jack, the Officer in Charge, he was a senior man ready for retirement, set in his ways with a quiet manner. In the summer of 1970/71, on a weekend, about twenty or so motor cyclists, Harley Davidson riders, members of a patched well-known Club, the 'Hells Angels' rode into the town. Jack and I were on duty. So, Jack in his wisdom, and I the new boy, approached the group lined up in the main street. Jack suggested that he do the talking. It is well known that this Club and the Police members were not friends so wisdom in our approach was the order of the day. All we did was talk to them to enquire after their intentions in the area, softly, softly.

Just outside of Mannum, part way to Murray Bridge was a tourist camping area, the Mannum waterfalls. The motorcycle group's intention was to camp there for the weekend for a break. Jack was satisfied with their attitude especially towards us, as he presented to them a non-aggressive attitude of friendliness. So, we left them to it.

The next day Jack and I drove out to the waterfalls, to check on them, to find that they were just lying around in a large group surrounding a stack of cartons of beer enough to get them all drunk. They actually welcomed our visit as we spoke to several of the members who assured us that they were not looking for trouble and just wanted to enjoy a relaxing weekend in great surroundings.

This event was an education for me as to Jack's attitude and methods and the way to achieve good relationships, so I give credit him and to that motorcycle Club. I must admit I was quite apprehensive and almost fearful not having had any experience with a Club of this nature.

On another general patrol of the area Jack and I went to Bow Hill east of Mannum, a small outpost on the river's edge about 12 km's distant, a general store and a few houses or holiday shacks. More credit to Jack in his policing attitudes. We borrowed a rowboat and crossed the river to an aboriginal camp. This was a new experience for me to see how some of our aboriginal people not integrating into our society, lived. A bark hut with a family of an aboriginal woman a white man and child, in very poor conditions. Our reason for visiting them was to check on their welfare, with no condemnation, but compassion. All part of Police work in a small country Station.

At a particular celebration party for the Car Club members, I made a serious error in judgement in making a comment to another person, which was totally offensive and consequently I was asked to leave the Club. This was very inappropriate as I was actually intoxicated, and as the local Policeman, became very unpopular, the whole thing to my regret.

This is where Kevin did the wrong thing by me as my work partner. The way it was done was not according to the general rules of police offences, but behind my back. He did not speak to me at all about the incident, but had a letter sent to me from the Car club committee, requesting I attend a special meeting which indicating my expulsion.

The shock of it put me on the edge of a breakdown. It was like the end of my world, I almost collapsed as I realised the implications of my actions. I had to tell Pauline of course, and she became just as traumatised as I. We had no idea what to do and we went to a local solicitor to get advice, which was of course to face the music.

One other incident was added to my list of problems, and that was the fact that I was involved in playing men's basketball with a Murray Bridge club. One match was very rough where some of the opposing team members were force fouling, so this guy did it to me once too often. The reader here may recall my earlier comments on my retaliatory behaviour in conflict. Yes, this guy ended up on the floor. This event stopped me from ever playing sport again.

Not wishing to make excuses, you, may see my life being conditioned to much stress and aggressive behaviour. This, I acknowledge also in moments of arresting persons who are aggressive, where more force than may be necessary in repressing that individual. My moral attitudes were failing badly.

The Mannum story brought much guilt and embarrassment to me, that I suffered a mental breakdown when on Holiday in Adelaide and the above events resulted in me leaving home and driving, with our dog, to Newcastle in New South Wales via Melbourne and Sydney and then driving back home over a week later. I blew off steam, and really wanted to disappear and not go back, but that little bit of love for my family had me phone Pauline and explain to her I would call again and come home. This I did. Our relationship strengthened as a result of this trauma which lasted over quite a period of time. Thankfully, the Department did not know anything of this.

I now know that extreme stress over incidences for any person does cause many to crack and commit serious crimes. I was fortunate that my God in Jesus Christ was in control and I recovered but with wounds. This of course happened before my spiritual transformation explained in the next Chapter, but just here I was just a member of the Uniting Church in Mannum. Today this form of mental illness is called 'Post traumatic Stress Disorder', which many returned servicemen do suffer, and receive counselling. That is help I never knew existed, so did not receive any.

I had made other mistakes, where wisdom was not a part of my thought patterns, so in delving into my mindset, I realise conscience was not there either.

On a very positive note, our daughter Jolie was born there in Mannum. We lived in a street which sloped downhill, conveniently to the Hospital. Pauline started labour pains in the evening of this particular day, and at about 1.30am her water broke. Our neighbour's daughter (who was Adrian's sitter) was woken and she baby sat Adrian while we got into the car to drive to the Hospital. I then realised that the fuel tank showed 'empty'. I hoped we would make it, and by the grace of God, we did. We coasted the car down the street across the main road into the Hospital driveway. There's more. We walked into the empty hospital, spoke to a nurse where Pauline was then taken into a birthing room and placed on a barouche. You may recall I was a cigarette smoker, so I walked out into corridor and lit up, shaking nervously. The nurse phoned the local Doctor while Pauline surprised the nurse and I when we heard a baby crying. I had only smoked half of the ciggie. The Female Doctor arrived and after examining both mother and baby, said "That is the easiest $40 I have ever earnt." She just checked them over and admitted them into a ward for the night. Now we had a beautiful baby daughter, Jolie, to look after, and so we settled down to a slightly larger family.

After all the mess-ups, our move away from Mannum arrived. As a conclusion to this section, I need to mention the effect on Pauline these incidences of negativity may have had. Of course, it was distressing for her, but she was strong and seemed to hide her emotions well, so we stayed close as a team in support of each other. It was a forced transfer back to the city, so we rented an apartment while our house was being built in the southern suburbs of Adelaide.

Motor Sport

This section is an introduction to the Mannum Car Club which really started my emotional difficulties psychologically. There is a secondary reason for this section, as being part of the car club, my actions brought about the problems I will be relating to.

While in Port Pirie I bought a 1954 Vanguard Spacemaster, a heavy English vehicle, which I remembered from my teenage years having driven one. So, I set about removing the body to rebuild it into a sports car, a dream of course which I took hold of. To make the body I obtained lengths of half inch 'oxy' pipe, which was a soft iron pipe used in the Port Pirie smelters for blowing oxygen into the furnaces. The pipe, being soft was perfect for bending and welding to form a body on the car, which I made covering the frame with sheets of galvanised iron. This did not happen until we moved to Mannum. The four-cylinder Vanguard engine I moved back behind the front suspension cross member to lower the centre of gravity.

The work went on incomplete when I had my transfer organised and a date set. I was still in the process of changing the engine mounts, and here I mention I had never welding anything before in my life, and with only a few clues from a friend, I did my best, but with painful results of welding flash eye damage. Not a good result, and lessons learnt. My eyes were experiencing the pain, where I was continually 'crying'.

The 'buggy' was towed to Mannum from Port Pirie behind our small

Toyota wagon, with my eyes streaming with tears and wearing the obligatory sunglasses. A trip I do not want to repeat. The bodywork on the vehicle was completed in the backyard of our Mannum Police house.

In the Mannum competitions, I destroyed two Vanguard engines, they were Ferguson tractor engines actually, 4-cylinder sloggers, and not up to punishing off road work. As I result, I came across and was given a powerful 1938 Dodge 6-cylinder engine and gearbox by a senior gentleman who lived on the Purnong Road. With the engine came new pistons rings and big end bearings. I had fitted this engine at about the time of the transfer and finished restoring it at our new home in O'Halloran Hill.

It was mobile and so I after moving to O'Halloran Hill, south of Adelaide, I joined the Southern District Car Club at Woodcroft. So, I continued to compete with the vehicle in Competition.

I mention this here, as the vehicle ended up being only slightly competitive but interesting to drive on the Club circuit, as the dodge engine proved to be an asset. The mechanic who assisted me in fixing the engine, said "I am amazed that this old engine revs so hard." For one year I was motorkhana director organising events at the Club grounds in Woodcroft. Being a member in the Club I settled into a good hobby which I enjoyed. Pauline showed some interest but had the children to look after, so only went with me to a few events.

The buggy was always parked in the driveway at our house and was not used for a season of rain, and when I went to start the engine, it wouldn't, it was seized. Water had seeped through from the spark plugs into the valve stems. Being a side valve engine, it would have been too hard to unseize, so I towed it to the dump and left it there. A sad day indeed. This was the end of my motor sport career.

This story may not be of too much interest to some people, but I have related it to indicate the stresses of where I was pushing myself, with building our house and the work in building retaining walls around the house. I know that the nature of establishing our nest, that every person does the same. So, this in itself is not unusual, but maybe my mindset did not cope well with these stresses, so as time went on, I developed a stress release by, as Pauline would say 'yelling' or raising my voice in order to get my way. This did not help our relationship. Adding to this was my attempts to stop smoking ciggies which did add to my attitudes. I was getting to emotional blow-up points on some occasions. While working in the Police Operations room I would smoke a packet an eight hour shift apart from the rest of my day. I would change from packets to rollem's to a pipe and back again.

Psychologically, when we are quiet, sitting meditating we need something to do with our hands, so for me, I lit up.

7

That Quiet Voice

In 1972, Pauline and I and our two little charmers moved back to Adelaide and rented a flat at St Mary's. I may have said earlier that we bought a block of land at O'Halloran Hill when we were engaged for $1500, which was only about 5km from where we rented the flat, as it turned out. While at Mannum I had a large 6m x 6m shed built on the block to store what I needed, and then, after we moved, we set about contracting a builder to build the house on the land for our future and to raise the children. We were fortunate that Pauline's cousin was a builder and so we employed him to build the house. The block, 25m x 120m, had a 20m slope diagonally, as a result the house was split level 2 ways which made for a house of interesting design, and being about a 425 square metre floor plan. Considering the year, in a gradually increasing economy, it cost us about $12,000. The equivalent now being about $150-200,000. At the end of that year, the house was finished, and we moved in, with a large amount of work for me to do in cementing paths and building numerous retaining walls, which I completed 2 years later. I became very fit indeed, hand mixing cement for the driveway and shed, and then man handling 45 ton of Carey Gully stone for the walls, about 60 meters of them some being about 1500mm high.

Here we have, a picture of our lives in this new era, area, and lifestyle, as a family settling into City and suburban life, in which we are still now engaged.

In the work area. I was attached to a Police reserve group employed in different relief areas of mainly patrols, such as hotel visits with cage cars waving the flag among the patrons. In this social area, the groups of people in the hotels bar areas were always rather lively, so in one hotel, 4 of us walked in through the bar, and then of course the murmur and the raised voices of disapproval rang out. One of the young men in a group turned around and actually abused us; his mistake; as I walked up to him, grabbed him by the collar and arrested him for offensive language. Not only were my comrades shocked at my immediate response, but so were the other members of the group as I marched him out of the hotel. Just another example of Police work, but a positive one for my self-esteem.

Pauline grew up in the Uniting Church, and during our courtship, I went along to her Church with her family, and so in our country postings I tagged along in those congregations. So, once we moved into our new home which was that only a few hundred meters away from the local Congregational Church we became attached there. We enjoyed our time there and gained many friends, some of whom we still spend time with. There was a small congregation there, and the Pastor/Minister, Harold, was a short stocky man of about 40 years of age, a modern man who wore a large beard. We became involved in this Christian body, and I took on the job of the church newsletter production with another member. Looking back from the current technological age with computers and mobile phones, I smile at the ancient technological machines we used in the 1970's. A

Gestetner machine was the in thing then, which I needed to use. It consisted of a dual sheet carbon copy which was typed upon, and the carbon copy was then fed through the Gestetner, where I could run off several copies. These small booklet newsletters were then distributed to the members on Sunday mornings.

Taking a step back for a moment and relating my experiences in the Christian Church during my late teenage years, apart from me being confirmed Anglican, I also went along to the local Baptist church, as invited by friends I met during this time through our sporting events, where we played in Inter Church basketball and tennis matches. I actually did a bible study course there with other youth, possibly with the objective of the Baptism in the denomination. Once again, I did not privately read the Bible, nor own one.

Hypocrisy was the order of the day, being teenagers, we were learning the ways of relationships, which, going by the memory of our doings, were in opposition to what we were taught. I won't go into detail as it is all part of growing up apart from the fact that relationships with the fairer sex were experimental.

Having met a young lady through the normal channels, I was very impressed with her and we dated and went out together a few times. Unfortunately, I had that drive where I needed to test the way the wind was blowing and failed miserably. She was a committed Salvation Army girl. In the meantime, I went with her to a few meetings, and was impressed with the totally different style of Christian worship and commitment. This 1960's era was when the Army walked the streets of the City with their musical talents singing Gospel songs as was their evangelical style.

Considering what I had been seeing within the Christian church and learning the Christian dogma, it had no effect on me, it was just part of life and appeared to be the expected normality. My knowledge was just being expanded but with no actual effect to my attitudes and lifestyle. Pure religion for the sake of being religious. A problem in society even today. It is obvious then, that in not actually knowing who Jesus is, and not reading the Bible, and living by the teachings therein, that there was no commitment to Him, but was only a surface show of religiosity.

The Miracle...May 1975

The Uniting Church, once per year, had, in this era, a special Stewardship weekend by having a Friday night dinner of the particular diocese followed by a special Sunday service. This event is the encouragement for paying the Tithe, which is a scriptural requirement of committing to donating one tenth of a person's income by a weekly financial gift for the purpose of supporting the Church organisation and the wages of the minister.

Pauline and I went to this Friday night dinner, attended by a large number of patrons, and at the opening of the evening meal a member stood up to say grace, and said:

"When I accepted Jesus Christ into my heart as Lord of my life......"

Suddenly, like a bolt of lightning, my eyes lit up and opened wide, as in all the years of service in the Church I had never heard those words spoken. These words stayed with me until the Sunday Service which we attended. I actually told Pauline of that eye-opening statement.

That morning, the service was much the same as usual, except that the form of service spoke to me directly, the hymns, the bible readings, the sermon, it all had an emotional effect on me which built up to the point that I felt like screaming. I had trouble controlling my emotions, my body was shaking, and I just wanted to get out of there quick. When the service ended, there was the usual line up at the front door with the people wanting to shake the Minister's hand on their way out. This was holding me up and I was shaking with impatience as I really needed to talk to him, not knowing what was happening to me. When I got to him, I grabbed his hand and asked him to take me somewhere quiet, as I needed him urgently. We went into a side room of the building, and I immediately fell on my knees, crying like a baby, pouring out my grief at my life not being able to cope. I asked Jesus to help me and come into my life right there. He did.

"Amazing Grace, how sweet the sound, that saved a wretch like me,
I once was lost, but now I am found,
T'was blind but now I see,
T'was Grace that taught my heart to fear, and Grace, my fears relieved,
how precious did that Grace appear the hour I first believed...."
Amazing Grace: John Newton, Circa 1700

Once I had calmed down and regained my composure, I walked outside with Harold to meet Pauline. All of the crowd had gone, and I told her that the load from my back had gone. I felt free and relaxed, with an air of joy over me as I felt the life of the sunshine warming over me. I told her that I had asked Jesus into my life. Harold was overjoyed, and he appeared bewildered, as I am not sure if this had happened to him before.

The freedom I felt was akin to the experience of the Pilgrim in the book I had read as a teenager, 'The Pilgrim's Progress.' He was walking to a goal along a wide road carrying a load on his back like a backpack. Along the way he had a choice of two paths, one was to continue along the wide easy road, the other, the narrow hard road. He chose the hard road and eventually got to his destination where that load was taken from his shoulders. This story I believe, was the Christian walk to the point of accepting Christ and following Him, and the hard path experienced to get there. So, my experience was exactly the same. When I read the book, it did not relate to me at that stage in my life, so in all of my young years my eyes were blinded to the truth of the Bible, as I now understand it was not my time to meet Him.

During the service, a young man was dedicated for service in Karratha in Western Australia working with the Aboriginal people there. Harold called for the Congregation to support him if they were able, so after Harold prayed for me, I gave him the money that I had in my wallet for that young man. It was a conviction, and a test of my resolve in my faith and change of heart.

That money was meant to replace the vinyl roof on my car during the forthcoming week, so I sacrificed that need for the man's ministry support. Later that week I kept the appointment, and the roof on the car was paid for, somehow. The Lord must have honoured my giving. Not only that, but I threw my pack of ciggies and my lighter in the bin as a commitment to stop my tobacco reliance. From that day until sometime later I did not smoke another ciggie. Also, during my life I had always chewed on my fingernails where they were shortened considerably, assuming that this habit is due mainly to nervous tension. On receiving the peace of our Lord Jesus, this habit has no longer any influence and has gone forever. Fingernails have become useful.

The story continues; our neighbours, aka Don and Donna, who we were very friendly with, had themselves recently become Christians and experienced similar release from their own difficulties, and shared with us about two other Christian experiences which were prominent in the Bible.

I share these Scriptures.

John 3.16, "For God had so much love for the world that he gave His only Son, so that whoever has faith in Him, may not come to destruction but have eternal life."

John 1. 31-33. "I myself had no knowledge of Him, (Jesus), but I came giving Baptism with water so that He might be seen openly by Israel………but He who sent me to give baptism with water said to me, 'The one on whom you see the Spirit coming down and resting, it is He who gives baptism with the Holy Spirit'."

So, after studying several other verses, Pauline and I were convinced that we should be baptised in water by immersion, (by Jesus example of dying to oneself, and rising up into new life,) and to be filled with the Holy Spirit where there is a sign as a witness of speaking in a spiritual language given by Father God. As a result, we both attended their Church and after a week I was baptised in water. The experience was such that I cried out for the infilling of the Holy Spirit, which did not happen then. It was explained to me, that by honouring God in this way, we are anointed with the power and authority of the name of Jesus the Christ.

Since the time of my being born again, (the person who accepts Christ and is 'saved' from himself and his ungodly life), I gradually slipped back into smoking ciggies, but only a few now and then. After my baptism in water, I have never smoked another cigarette, except to light one for someone else, and my health problem of waking up coughing every morning, no longer affected me. I was able to breathe deeply as Jesus had totally cleaned out my lungs of cigarette tar, this was immediate as I had smoked a ciggie prior to entering that Church.

The next week we went again with Don and Donna, and I went forward for the infilling of the Holy Spirit along with about twenty other persons to the front of the Church, but the Pastor praying for me, (as I know now) was not anointed and was not truthful, as I knew nothing was happening. How did I know? Firstly, as he said the words, "I sense you are coming through now, you are coming through." I just knew I wasn't.

Secondly when I went back to my seat, there were a number of people who were surrounding Pauline, and she appeared threatened by them all and intimidated. We never went back to that Church. So, God used that fellowship for bringing about part two of my Christian experience.

A New Walk Starts

Pauline and I, with Adrian and Jolie, continued attending the Uniting Church for a while, until other events changed that. In the meantime,

Pauline, being pregnant with our third child, was getting near to that time of release. Life was getting busy.

Pauline's mother, a widow, being in the past a dedicated Uniting Church person, had been attending an Apostolic/Pentecostal Church in the City, the Christian Revival Crusade, and as a result of my experience she suggested we attend the Bethesda Church at Marion, an affiliated body. This we did, and we were astonished at the level of love and joy of worship in that Church, the vast difference in the number of people in the congregation, and their very different attitudes and affection. This we saw was a real body of Christ. We were introduced to Pastor Bob McGregor, one of the leadership team, and a young family of our age. We were also invited by a Senior Pastor Charles and Mavis Schwab to their home for a meal. He said that they did this every Sunday with new people. This did show us the honesty and genuineness of the people there. They were real.

We continued to attend both Churches for quite a while, until we learnt that Pastor Bob and the young family, Phil and Pam Murphy, were happy to come to our home and discuss the Baptism of the Holy Spirit with us and pray for us. Pauline was sceptical and we disagreed to a point on this matter, as she was unsure, considering her Uniting Church background. When she was 14 years old, she had accepted Jesus as her Lord at a Billy Graham crusade in Adelaide, and she was certainly firm in her convictions, to her credit. (That's why I loved her so much.)

We had that meeting in our home, and, as we already knew the scriptural references, it didn't take much discussion as I related the experience, I had with the other Charismatic Church which we had left four months earlier. So, the group prayed for both of us, and immediately I burst out in total joy, speaking in an unknown babbly language, the anointing of which was so strong that I nearly fell over, laughing and holding onto the mantel piece in the lounge room. The feeling was so ecstatic that I was just totally overcome with the warmth of that Holy Spirit anointing. An experience I will never forget, and one which is beyond just a moment but for the rest of my life. It was a prayer language of praise to God, and an ability to hear his voice when He calls. Pauline saw my reaction under the anointing, and she received the gift at the same time and spoke in her new language in praise. We were totally ecstatic.

So, we were both suddenly released into a stronger bond of fellowship due to this triune experience of salvation, May 1975, baptism in water by immersion in November 1975, and the infilling of the Holy spirit in February 1976.

We then continued in fellowship within this church body and later, it's satellite church nearer our home for over 30 years.

8

Another Vice Gone

Just one other matter at this time, which needed dealing with. I loved my glass of red wine, a shiraz claret, from my not quite distant family of Redman's Coonawarra winery which was my favourite. My love of red wine came from an experience while stationed at Mannum, where I attended a wine flagonning and BBQ at the Waikerie Winey. The local Jaycee's organised a trip there for an evening visit and I, the local Policeman, was invited. I drove a carload of friends from Mannum to Waikerie and one of the men took the responsibility of the reserve driver who did not partake. Anyway, a few of us, including our Jaycee rep and I got paracletic, drinking schooner glasses of claret. Mistake! Eventually, after a very happy evening, our sober driver got us home, as I tried but was so drunk, I threw up.

The lesson was that I kept a liking for red wine, until after my Holy Spirit experience, when I was drinking one small glass of wine per evening, which extended after a month or so to two glasses per evening. One night when we had friends at our house, Dean said to me… "How can you worship God with a mind dulled with alcohol."

What a wake-up call! I was getting close to alcoholism, as I recognised, I was being drawn away from my new-found change in life, it was like taking the blinkers off. From that day, I stopped drinking alcoholic drinks and was released from any addiction which I may have been heading to. As the years have gone by, I never had a problem with the occasional glass of wine or beer, but only under the occasion of meal outings. I never stocked up again. So, over this period, I was released from my habits, where they were affecting my health and wellbeing. I may seem simplistic, but from this era, my health has been improved considerably. I can breathe deeply and have never again suffered from drunkenness.

There was one other experience resulting from that Baptism. I was at home a day or so later, and I looked over the valley from our home at O'Halloran Hill, and for the first time in years I saw the scenery in 3D. That scenery I was seeing with different eyes. What had happened to me throughout the renewal of Spirit, was to be more aware of the depth of God's creation.

God had renewed my heart to see His creation with His eyes as to its beauty. The appreciation of our world was increased to being thankful to Him for putting us in this beautiful location.

Alienation

Back to the Uniting Church, considering my 'conversion' to a greater lifestyle in Christ, I spoke to the Minister there and told him what had happened since he prayed for me in his office; he appeared to not understand what had happened as it did not fit his theological perceptions, and especially with the Holy Spirit baptism, all he could say was....

"Don't you ever speak in tongues in my Church". He said with authority...

It was obvious to us that our time within the Uniting Church was over, and so we never went back there and continued to enjoy the life within the Bethesda Movement of Pentecostal churches. Although we left that small Congregational Church, we stayed with some of the friends we made there, and still see them to this day.

The time had now come for Pauline to give birth to another beautiful daughter, Kylie, to complete our family. It was interesting to note that she was born in this transition period in our lives with new friends and a more spiritual lifestyle. I do believe that, knowing what we know now, Kylie, being born at this time, carried an anointing, where her personality has given her a maturity and joyful attitude, at the same time being raised not only by us, but her siblings, who were much older than her, 12 years younger than Adrian, and 8 years younger than Jolie. This has now shown in her missionary role with her husband Daniel, and other friends, now living in Hobart, that they are the leaders in their own Christian fellowship, and also that she is a trained counsellor in that fellowship.

I was employed in the Police Operations room at the time of my salvation, having been there for some time. Paul, one of the operators on our team, had become a Christian some time previously, and he was full of verve and was quite a happy chappie, so we got on well. I was a capable member, and the other men, as a team, shared the tasks and rotated from the 'phones', taking calls from the public as directed by the general switchboard, for the purpose of tasking the mobile patrols to any of a large number of incidences requiring their attention. The other area of rotation took place in the operator booth directing the patrols. I was average, until Jesus changed me, and a peace and confidence overtook me to be a reliable and competent booth operator, where I could multi-task. The job in the booth was to remove a job card from the conveyer sent by the men on the phones, give the job on the card to the patrol, then on the completion of that job, receive and record the results and return the card to the team sergeant for filing. I was able to do all those 3 things at once for the different jobs that passed through my hands.

At the time of my resignation, as will be seen, that was reversed, so something of my mindset changed during the next 10 years.

Attitude changes between my peers and I were becoming quite noticeable now, due to my mindset change from a blasphemer and smoker to a much more righteous cleanskin. My conversation and work abilities altered due to that newfound peace. I, and also Paul, him being much louder than I, would pour out our new life to the others in the operations room, as is natural to a Christian. The responses from the others did create contrary discussions to the point when it could be taken as persecution. Our acceptance was declining. For me it became positive when the team realised that my talents in the room blossomed into respect, but for that reason only. This by itself was a testimony.

After two years being stationed in the Police Operations room, soon after my conversion, I applied for a transfer to the Driver Training section at Thebarton Barracks, and I was accepted after completing a two-week instructor's course. This was one of my best postings, as I believed that I had higher than usual driving skills and was glad to be able to pass on those skills on to students for entry into the Police Department. (I had taught all of our 3 children to drive efficiently with confidence.) This is where persecution started in me not being accepted as a Christian, due to the ego of a few other long time Instructors, and their lack of trust in my abilities. It was from here that I was transferred to Darlington 2 years later.

Some instructors were OK, but there were a few of the senior men that continually harassed me and heckled me which did not afford me the privilege of being issued with a motorcycle for personal transport to and from the workplace. The other Instructors did have that privilege. I had no trouble in passing the Instructors Course, as my driving ability was quite fearless and accurate. My acceptance during the course was not a problem, until I was on the road teaching students. I admit I made mistakes, but my skills from past private experience endeared me with the students. I frightened them actually, when demonstrating what I wanted them to do. The problem with the other Instructors was that they took the divine peace that I had as a lack of aggressiveness, almost carelessness, towards being dangerous. So, I was not trusted, even while producing very good results in the students improved driving capabilities. I received so much criticism that eventually, after 2 years, I needed to be transferred.

9
Church Life

Having settled into a new life within the Pentecostal Christian church, much relearning of how the body of Christ expressed the love of God was shown, which was over and above the observation of the religiosity of the mainstream church which we had grown up in. In other words, we saw the power and anointing of the Pentecostal movement, which the mainstream church did not have. We came into this stream where, in the 1970's and 80's, large meetings were held around Adelaide and Australia in public venues. Pastoral teams, who carried the anointing of healing, evangelism, and teaching, would visit these meetings from overseas. Other ministers within Australia would work with them. We saw biblical scripture put into practice with these ministries with life changing results for many people. There are multitudes of books written by these ministers of worldwide renown. Part of these learning experiences showed us the whole body of Christ worldwide, where the mainstream church appeared localised.

In summarising, a massive change in the knowledge and understanding of the whole body of Christ worldwide, which was hidden from view until I committed myself to Him.

Bible College

In 1979, the Bethesda movement, which controlled several satellite cells or church bodies, held a 6 month in house bible college course, and I was encouraged to apply. The course was held in the upstairs rooms of the church building. There were 14 Students, and 12 or more lecturers, some from other countries, one of whom was the apostle of the largest church in the world in Korea of over one million adherents, Pastor David Yonggi Cho. Having served in the police department for 16 years, I was entitled to some long service leave, and also the yearly annual leave of 6 weeks. This time covered the 6-month period of the college.

Many close relationships were developed within that time, especially with the church Leadership. Much was learnt in bible surveys and studies, under a lecture environment. Practical applications of the teaching took us to a new level of ministering with much personal teaching experience sharing with the group. The presence of the Holy Spirit was there in power as we prayed for each other under guidance of the lecturers. One afternoon of note was when I prayed one of the students suffering a headache. He was immediately healed as I laid hands on him, a minor part of the evidence of that Holy spirit anointing, but evidence none the less. The musical talents within the group were melodious in leading us all into worship of our Lord, which was a large part of the presence of love and commitment among the group. A major part of the course was our service to the community, where, due to the establishment of a coffee lounge in Hindley Street in the city, we would cruise on foot, the area of Hindley St and Rundle Mall inviting young people to the lounge. This was very successful in introducing Jesus to those who frequented this street which was Adelaide's coffee lounge and nightclub strip. We did share the gospel of Jesus Christ to many people over a period of two months every Friday night in that area. It was a time of confidence building for me and others in the group. In fact, two young people that I know of did accept Christ during this time.

At the end of the 6-month period of college, the church held a graduation ceremony for us all, and yours truly bought a new suit for the occasion. For me personally, this was a very poignant time of achievement in my life, where for 6 months, I spent the time with total Christian company. Of interest, during the college time, I let my hair down literally, due to the dress requirements in the police department, clean shaven etc, I grew long hair, a beard and moustache. I didn't know myself. Also, once I outgrew my suit, I never again wore one, let alone a tie....

So, I can testify that, in then returning to life back in the workforce and non-Christian people, the impact was almost overwhelming due to the spiritual vacuum in 'that' world. This, I believe, is what is said to be the difference within the body of Christ, to label it, the church, and the world.

The Pain of Blasphemy

I give an example. In the first year of becoming 'born again', Pauline and I went to a roman catholic charismatic service, in the city, with a new family of friends from Bethesda. The service was being led by a nun dressed in her habit as was the custom. Behind her stood a man, who I thought was to be introduced by her as the pastor. But not so, the nun led the whole service. I realised later that the catholic doctrine was that the nun must have male covering, the reason for him being there behind her.

Also, during a prayer, the nun mentioned praying to the virgin Mary. That prayer hit me so hard that I felt stabbing pains in my chest as if a heart attack. It really hurt as I almost bent over holding my chest. I later recognised that her prayer could have been blasphemous.

I experienced this same pain, the very day I returned to work from bible college, when, while having lunch in the police cafeteria, one of the men I had been working with walked over to the table and made a comment laced with the name of Jesus Christ, as a word of abuse. The stabbing pain I then felt, as before, caused me to lean forward as I held my chest. That comment was obviously blasphemous.

With these two experiences, it was proved to me the absolute power of the name of Jesus, and that name if used as a swear word of abuse, no matter what one is doing within an environment where in the workplace or elsewhere, then the Christian is subject to hearing blasphemous statements, with the result that our spirit is harmed. This with the possibility of the dulling of our Christian walk which gives us a loss of power and ability to walk closely with our lord Jesus. I believe this is what happened to me.

A summary here, of the power and spiritual difference between the administration of the spiritual gifts separating two opposing belief systems.

Teacher

In 1980, as a result of my completing bible college, I took on the task of teaching in the youth area of the church, first- and second-year high school students. A worthy experience in teaching them of what I learnt in the college, and in my life. A sideline or two of this was that I worked under the youth pastor, where we organised weekend camps at a property in Melrose under a marquee to a large number of youths. The property was owned by the parents of a young woman who attended the church. There was a young teenager, female, who was somewhat rebellious, 14 years old, and a victim of parental instability. She adopted me as her father, and over several years, I ministered to her as a daughter into a stable young woman. It appeared to me that this form of ministry was easy for me. I was involved with this teaching at the church for 2 years until a satellite church was established in Morphettville, and for 4 years I led a group of mature volunteers within the fellowship along with Pauline, to run the Sunday school consisting of primary school children.

This Church grew substantially under several leadership changes of good repute, until unfavourable conditions forced Pauline and I and our 3 children to leave after 33 years. Pauline and I were totally devastated by the events under the poor leadership of the pastor at this time, which affected us emotionally for the amount of time we had put into this community. We had made many friends, it was a mature body of believers, but, over the three years under the new pastor, many drifted out, reducing the numbers by over half. I recall seeing one beautiful couple leave the church building in tears one morning, so I only assume that other couples left similarly. The changes to us were related to the worship music which verged on hard rock and was not acceptable to us and we were not listened to when we complained.

This occurred over a period of about a year. I found that it was almost impossible to worship the lord, at different times, and so needed to leave the meeting and wait outside until it was over. Then one morning I just lost it, screamed for the pastor to stop and walked out. It actually hurt my spirit. He was a guitarist and the worship leader, and the music he used included a playing method of 'reverb', a noise which is a continuous repeat of one note loudly.

After the meeting Pauline and I had a talk with the pastor and two friends of ours who were part of the pastor's team in his office, explaining that his music was a problem. He ignored my complaint anyway. The other two men apparently were not offended by our actions, as we are still on friendly terms with them.

We then told the pastor we must leave. This was very hard to do and we left in tears. We took time out for two or three days and went north to the Flinders Ranges to recuperate. God's word was the order of the day as we surrendered to his plans for us. This brought about a new level of spiritual growth.

Although, at the time, these circumstances were devastating, we realise that God used them for the better good and to take us to a higher level. Some years before Pauline had attained a diploma in library studies at TAFE, meaning that she now held a title of library technician. While at the Bethesda South church, under previous strong leadership, one of the members there started a small bible college and Pauline built a library there for the college and the church. Unfortunately, after a period of time the college did not survive for administrative reasons.

In the meantime, Pauline began employment in the Magarey and

Son's orchard in Coromandel Valley, as book keeper and office assistant under the oldest brother of 4, Hugh Magarey's, leadership. This continued until December 2017, when she retired. Hugh, with his wife Ruth, were adherents to the Australian house of prayer for all nations apostolic prayer ministry, under apostle Jenny Hagger and her team in the office at Aldgate in the Adelaide hills. Her employment meant that, with this church connection, she became involved in the office as librarian, being in charge of the resource room in that office, where she is still the manager, now for 20 years.

Youth with a Mission

Through Pauline's involvement with House of Prayer, her mentor Enid, mentioned that the Youth with a Mission base at Norton Summit, had formed a group of people called 'Friends of YWAM', and they were looking for volunteers to work on the property and many other areas.

The property was a 25-acre allotment on the eastern slope of the hilltop 5 km's into the close foothills of Adelaide. A large 3 storey house had been built on the property in 1863 as a private property initially and then a children's home in the 20th century. YWAM purchased the property in the 1990's.

I answered that call and joined the team on the old property at Norton Summit to put my building skills to work, and in the year 2000 I volunteered as a builder/handyman at the base part time, for the next almost 10 years. After the incident at the Morphettvale Church, we both then attended the small intercessory fellowship of Zion Hill, which consisted of a group of about 40 persons under Jenny Hagger's leadership, supporting her Ministry as a prayer group, and held

Sunday mornings. The meetings were held at Hahndort in the Resort there in a disused building. So, we both settled into a very loving group of people for prayer and worship. This happened in 2009.

As a result, Pauline and I became very good friends with Garry Parkinson and his family, who were involved in their particular role and ministry within that organisation, which included working with illegal immigrants, boat people, in that era. He would travel to Port Augusta to the army barracks there to work with them as they were attempting to integrate into our society by obtaining their particular visas. We were being social together in our fitness regime of walking about the area, as Garry was a big man, as I was becoming, and he always encouraged me to walk with him. In 2008, he and his family, wife Christie and 3 children, took on a ministry role as manager of a YWAM base in Perm, Russia. After a year, he was then posted to Krasnoyarsk in Siberia to start a base there. Within a few months he invited Pauline and I to work with him in that city.

Working at the YWAM base was a privilege, and even though I had many abilities in carpentry, metal and cement jobs, etc, these skills were honed as I was working with the regular man, and the base Manager Kris. Garry, of course, with his crass wit, blending with mine, always came along to check on my work. I had been finishing off a small shed outside the kitchen which housed the Rubbish bins. Garry, inspected my work and said: "Hey Graham, that timber's not straight, I thought you were a carpenter...."

"Thanks Garry, you're a real mate, I didn't put the posts in, you did that, didn't you?"

"Get lost," he replied laughing..... That was the start of a long-lasting friendship.

Over the years I spent there, I did quite large building maintenance jobs, construction and demolition included. The biggest were constructing roofs for two 100,000 litre concrete rainwater tanks and a timber split staircase between two levels to a house. I installed wall panels and windows to close in a verandah on the main house, converting it to a computer office for the students, and many other minor jobs. The best job was to co-ordinate the job of enlarging the dining room in the building, an old three storey mansion built in 1863, with 1m thick stone walls. The job, as a whole, was contracted to a Christian organisation, 'Mobile Mission Maintenance', and I assisted where required, and was the co-ordinator between MMM and Kris the manager of the organisation. This job took 3 months part time for the team and I, and I had the enviable task of demolishing the old stone wall and assisting with installing a 300mm steel I-beam across the width of the room which was to be supported by the external upstairs verandah. This job required the intervention of a structural engineer. The wall, I tackled with a heavy jackhammer horizontally, and took two days.

After Garry and his family left for Russian ministry for YWAM, I completed my work at that historical place, and he kept on my back for Pauline and I to go to Russia to help him with work over there.

10

Missions

China 1988

On the completion of my time in the Bible course at Bethesda in 1979, apart from being part of a helps, or, deacons' team, we became friends with many of the people in the fellowship eventually being part of the satellite home groups in the southern suburbs where we live. As a result, we were asked by Pam and Philip Murphy (Philip is now deceased) to join a team to go to China, on a missionary trip. A serious event where we were to take in Christian Bibles and literature to the Chinese Church. China, being governed by a Communist Government, are not happy with strong liberal Christian Churches, so any import of this literature is not well received. The Government does allow the Christian religion but is sponsored by the Government.

Therefore, a group of twelve male and female Christian people, including Pauline and I, took up the challenge and headed for China via Hong Kong, the year was 1988. We stayed for 1 week in Hong Kong, preparing for the trip into the mainland, being schooled into how to do the job, prayerfully fitting in with God's plans.

I relate one incident which created a stir among the group, which was of great concern, and occurred when we visited the Victoria Peak, The Peak Lookout. We stayed together as a group, but due to the circular style of the tower we were separated, I walked the loop looking for Pauline when I suddenly realised, I was alone. I even went outside onto the road looking for the group to no avail. I had no idea where they went, there appeared to be nowhere to go from the bus stop there. The lookout was deserted. I thought they had gone and left me behind. I had no choice but to catch a taxi back to the hotel where we were staying. Very soon after I arrived at our room, the phone rang, I answered it and it was Philip on the other end. The group had been looking for me and even had advised the police. He then told me, as I explained what happened.

"We had walked up the stairs outside at the end of the building to go up to another lookout, sorry Graham, we thought you were with us."

"That's ok Phil, as I couldn't find you, I thought it best to go to the hotel. I didn't see any walkway to the top." I replied very apologetically.

God is always in control and had inspired us to use wisdom in planned action.

At the end of our stay in Hong Kong, we travelled across the bay in the underground train, to the railway station in the new territories to cross the border into mainline china. I was amused being in this train under the bay, as it is an eight-car vehicle packed with black haired Chinese people, so with me being 6 foot tall I could see over the top of a mass of black heads as the train appeared as a caterpillar snaking along its track.

God in Control

Our first trip into the Mainland, was a test trip really, a day trip, where we packed our travel shoulder bags with bibles and literature, just one item of clothing and a newspaper on top, which was designed to hide the contents from searches, which does not necessarily prevent discovery. What it did was, if one of the team were searched, it removed suspicion from the remainder of the group who were interspersed throughout the crowd.

We all boarded the train, well prepared, and, on passing through Customs, none of us were searched thankfully. What happened next was that we walked into a large area with seating not quite out in the open, but I was concerned as we were isolated that we may have created suspicion if anyone was watching. We were approached by two young people carrying large sports bags. This is where the strength and protection of the Lord comes in. 12 of us emptied our bags into the two sports bags. Now, the weight of my bag was cutting into my shoulder. I watched in disbelief and awe, as this young man and his female companion, left us carrying that huge weight six times what I had been carrying, we prayed for them as they went. We learnt later that all of that literature had been distributed under an hour later.

The Border Crossing

Before leaving Hong Kong, we packed our bags by stacking our Bibles and literature vertically in the cases, so when passing them through the Customs Xray machines it all appeared as straight lines.

We all took our time holding back once we alighted from the train and approached the Customs area. To our delight we were ushered through without any checks at all, the Xray machine was shut down.

One more amusing incident. We were approached by a guide, who in his wish to please, picked up my bag, and said with his Chinese accent,

"What have you got in here? Books?"

I could hardly control myself in trying to hide my laughter at this statement, I said to Pauline, "If only he knew...".

Our taxi to the hotel was a minivan into which only 6 of us plus baggage would fit. The driver then showed us his racing skills as a driver, even so we made it. Upon reaching our rooms, this James Bond smuggling team, under tight security, off loaded our Library into the room next door to whoever was there then took it all with them. We were told that the material was distributed within 30 minutes. A successful expedition completed.

We entered the country as tourists and visited several cities led by a Chinese guide in a minibus, staying in 4-star hotels. We visited Shanghai and the Bund, where we were 'accosted' by about 100 young people wanting to be sponsored to Australia to study in our universities, one young man pleaded with me in tears.

This was on a Sunday; the crowd of young people was no surprise, and the area was totally jam packed with people out walking. Concertina buses were overflowing with people also try to get to their destination. People trying to get on would push people into the bus and then hang on somehow.

Beijing was next, where we toured the Great Wall, walking some distance along same. It was a 1-hour bus trip from Beijing, to a large gate and shops or offices embedded, and the parking area was crowded with many buses. The walk on the wall was steep and hard work, a wide walk but well worth the effort. The views from the wall were astonishing.

The Li River tour, where 40 boats each carrying 75 people glided down the beautiful river to its destination small town. Buses were waiting there to take us back to our hotel. We were supplied with a meal along the way, and I noticed that the meals were prepared by two women in the rear of the two-deck boat. They washed the greens in the clear river water from the back of the boat, which looked pure, but on the way down, travelling past villages on the banks of the river, I saw people and children swimming in the river, and water buffalo doing what they do. Also, the diesel exhausts from the chug a chug motor were mixing with the water. We all decided that we would not eat the greens.

On the way back we stopped in a village which was a large family quadrangle building, of adults and children. The people there were astounded that we should visit them, possibly as they had never encountered westerners before. They wanted to entertain us, but we needed to decline as these were poor Chinese farmers. With their permission, one of the group, took photos of the children with the instant camera and gave them to the parents. We handed them some Christian literature which we were carrying, as a gift which needed to be handed to them with two hands, indicating very valuable material, which they graciously received.

Back in the city, on a Sunday morning while we were walking across a bridge, we encountered a family walking in the opposite direction. The father was carrying a Bible and he proudly smiled at us and showed us his bible to indicate that they were going to church to worship.

We did the job we went there for, but it was time to return home. This trip was one year before the Tiananmen Square student demonstration massacre. Our trip was a total success.

India, 1999

The next Mission trip occurred while my family were attending the Morphettvale church, where Pastor Jo Jo Thomas and his wife were part of the fellowship having migrated from Kerala in south west India. Pauline was not up to this trip, as she may not have been able to cope with the humidity. A group of nine, including me left with Jo Jo and a team of seven others to go to his hometown in Kerala. We lived in his brother's house on a rubber plantation property on the side of a hill while there.

This was a trip to remember, or forget, depending on one's views. The object was to evangelise the area in his hometown but ended up with only one open air meeting with no known respondees. A very small group. Another meeting, which was arranged and was set up in a village with a stage and electrical amplification, for us to use, was taken over by the local politician. Two down one to go. Another village was much more receptive and productive, this was enjoyable, as Jo Jo needed to do the evangelising due to language, so this made our trip worthwhile. Nothing miraculous though. Kerala is a Catholic state in India, and Pentecostal churches were not welcome as we found out, when we went to the family church, a rented private house, from which the fellowship was eventually ejected.

We attended a meeting there where we were all guests and ministered to the people there. The house was crowded and segregated, and the people were very attentive. I was asked to pray for a young girl who had a club foot. I am not sure whether the girl actually wanted to be prayed for, as, when I laid hands on her and prayed in the Spirit, I was thrown back away from her and I hit my head on a window ledge. Had she wanted the prayer she perhaps would have fainted in the Spirit and may have been healed. A very interesting result.

Some highlights of the trip of interest here; the humidity at Kerala is extremely high in the south west, which is just 10deg above the equator, we travelled for 14 hrs from the Airport on our arrival in a commuter Leyland rattletrap bus to our destination. The Pastor of our church and his wife were sitting on the righthand side above the rear wheels, also where the diesel exhaust was. When we were near our village, his wife took her glasses off and to our dismay, but with laughter, her face was black with white circles for eyes, the pastor was the same. Their faces were covered in soot. These buses do not have windows. Unfortunately, the exhaust fumes caused her to contract bronchitis, and laid her up for a week. I came down with it as soon as I arrived back home.

Another experience had it's good and bad side, the good side was when we took a bus ride to an Australian dairy farm (The cattle were Australian) at the top of a huge mountain, to witness a Monastery dairy and its operation. The trip up in the bus was quite an experience as Pauline and I were seated on the left side seats, now she has a fear of heights, so I was sitting on the window seat looking almost straight down about 500 feet into a deep chasm. The trip down in the bus was a horror ride, for one hour winding down the side of this steep mountain with that vertical drop from the road, but this time on the mountain side of the road. Every time the driver would either brake or drive, the tail shaft would clunk. The further down the mountain we went the brakes would squeal getting worse after every corner. By the time we got to the bottom, they were screaming, no linings left. Indian 50-year-old Leyland Ashok buses. We made it by God's grace.

India was a fascinating place, very crowded, with vast differences, rich to poor, with a mix of modern and ancient practices, poor electric supplies, and the list goes on, a backward country trying to catchup really.

East Timor, 2004

Once again, through church contacts, and a sort of relative of mine and Pauline's, Graham May, we heard of a mission trip to East Timor, involving a work detail in villages near Dili, the capital of the country. It was organised through a mission organisation in Victoria, for a group here in South Australia. This came about after the devastation in Timor, when Indonesia invaded splitting Timor in two in 1991. The team was organised with two families in Mt Barker, myself, Graham and two others. Contact had already been made in East Timor where work needed to be done, and so the trip went ahead.

We all flew to Darwin, stayed the night in a church building and then flew in a light plane to Dili, a trip of about one hour. We were met by a local person and conveyed over a mountain to the village where we were to work.

My memory here is vague as to detail, especially names, so I will do a summary of this trip to indicate life in this community, and its rewards.

A tour of the area showed us the devastation of what were industrious areas and businesses, housing areas destroyed, and just general ruins. The vision was to assist to rebuild the village, with a school in a tribal village, a larger school in the town, and other works as required.

Our first job, which took almost our full time here, was in the tribal village a 15-minute trip from the town along a road following two creeks to get there. It was to assist with a water supply where the spring was quite putrid and needed cleaning. There was one tap in this village. The main job was to build a small School, as the population of the village consisted of many small children, old men and women, and men over 50 years of age who were the 'soldiers. They were grim men looking at us with suspicion, carrying machetes in their belt.

The one section of the population that we noticed was missing, here as in other villages, was the 20-50-year age group, these having been taken in war."

The school building's foundations were unique, it took 2 days for the team to build a mirror base of stones for the containment of a concrete pour for the actual footings. The walls were constructed of palm frond mats of some strength to be attached to the wall framing which were the usual 3 x 2 timbers bolted into the concrete. The roof was of corrugated iron, where John V, our roof man had great difficulty getting nails into the very hard dark red timbers.

The children in this village were fascinated with our group and we all enjoyed our time with these people. There was a ceremony put on by our town hosts and the village people, to our delight, for the job done.

Once completed, we went on a trip over the island to a town on the coast in two 4WD vehicles, one of which I drove. This trip was an eye opener as to the nature of the small towns on the way, where we needed to be wary of the townspeople, who were tribal, and, as before, the men carrying their machetes, eyeing us off with suspicion . We made sure we stayed in a group. On this trip my inferiority showed up. Graham, the team leader and I did not hit it off, even though we knew each other as relations, and also due to the fact we were all strangers having met only a few times, I volunteered to drive over the island. Graham insisted that locally he drive everywhere. My experience told me he was a lousy driver, so I attempted to take the reins where possible, but I was ignored. Even working on the school foundations, he had no idea in explaining how to build them, so he and I struggled. I was a mess emotionally here, in this situation.

I have always been interested in geology, and noted that the island, in totality, consists of huge rocks, boulders, stones, and gravel. The main large river in Dili, is totally large stones, gravel and sand. There is virtually no soil except on level ground. On the trip south we saw huge boulders of several hundred tons, and the whole area being as mentioned. On the road, we came across a huge landslide area where the steep mountainside slid away from about 500 feet above and over 500 feet down, taking the road with it. That mountain was built of pure rocks and no soil, meaning that was the makeup of the island, rocks, rocks, and more rocks. A perfect example of our great worldwide Noahic flood piling it all up from wherever.

I cannot recall any detail of this trip to the south coast now. We only stayed there for one night, before returning to the village near Dili, where a feast was put on for a School there where graduates were honoured. A pig on a spit was the order of the day. A very fitting tribute and a parting party for our trip home.

11

Russia

In July 2010 Garry sent us invitations from a support Church in the city for our Visas, and we then planned a trip to meet Garry in Krasnoyarsk. I believe that Garry was chosen to take to the mission field in Russia, as he had an attitude and joyful persona that had people attracted to him. He had a reputation for his ability to befriend people immediately, creating a trustworthy friendliness. So, we were amazed that this reputation went with him to Krasnoyarsk in October of that year, gather people to him to assist in setting up a YWAM base, then go on leave back in Australia from December until February. He then, on his return to the city forged a relationship with a large Christian, Russian Baptist church where he was able to gain letters of invitation for us to be sponsored in our visit to the country.

The visas were obtained from the Russian Consulate in Canberra, a very strict routine where we were required to have the trip and dates planned 2 weeks before the due date. Talk about nerves. We chose the quick application which cost us $400. Our trip plan, which was organised by a travel agent, was for travel with China Airlines, via Shanghai and Beijing, to Moscow. Then we would board the overland train to Krasnoyarsk, a trip of 3 days, which we did not need to do, but for me, being a train buff, a trip on the Siberian Express was a ride not to miss. The airports in China were huge, and easy to get lost in, especially in Beijing where we could not get an airport hotel and so slept on a bench. We arrived there at 1 am, for transfer to Moscow leaving at 7.30am.

An interesting anecdote here, on landing in Moscow, we climbed from the plane via a land bridge among a crowd of scurrying Chinese who had also been on our plane, they must have been in a hurry for some reason. We were able to read the Russian and English signage guiding us to the carousel for a distance along a corridor to collect our baggage. We then walked along another corridor and then down a staircase into a very small check in area of 5 check in security booths. The Chinese people and one other person, who appeared to Pauline and I, to be the only other European westerner on board. We were now faced with lining up at the booths, the Chinese people swarmed to the only open check in counter in a wedge. We were in the middle of the crush. The Russian security person in that booth sent only 3 or 4 people through and closed the booth. The adjacent booth was then opened by another Russian, and the crowd of Chinese swarmed to this booth. Then after very slow movement of people through that booth, the Russian then did the same thing after a few were passed through. Then another Russian man opened a booth the other side of the first, and that wedge of people stampeded to his booth to the extent that they knocked over the security bollards.

We 3 smiled at each other, and I said, as Pauline laughed, "I think we'll stay here, don't you?" Our travelling companion also laughed and said, "Yeah, I think so."

We three were chuckling away, as we were so amused at the obvious torment the officials were putting out onto the Chinese.

So, we stayed where we were, and we walked to the front of the line when that booth was reopened. I commented to the female booth operator and smiled, and she did the same. We passed through within seconds. The Russian operators I think, were playing with the hapless Chinese. I say this, not wishing to offend them, but to indicate a Russian attitude to them. This was a very amusing entry into Moscow, and we enjoyed every minute of it. Really, the security I thought was quite lax, there were no bag checks, only passport and identification checks done. The Russian security attendant, behind her screen looked at my passport, then at me as she scanned me, but with an amused, cheeky smile.

"Thank you, you may pass," she said in broken English, as I reclaimed my passport.

Pauline and I were very relieved to get through the check in, so after claiming our luggage we walked out into a huge area milling with people of all nationalities, we were met by a short stocky English woman, Wanda, who was part of the Moscow YWAM team, holding a sign with our name on it.

"Hello, Graham, hello Pauline, welcome to Moscow." There were big smiles all round, as we wheeled our luggage behind us to follow her out of the building to a waiting Transit Bus.

"Did you have a good flight guys?"

"Oh, yes," I quipped, "The best part from coming through the check in security." I related joyfully, the event with the shuffling Chinese passengers, to the chuckling woman.

"We will take this bus to near my apartment, then a bit of a walk there, through one of the poorer areas. Then tomorrow morning I will take you to the railway station, it's only a short walk." She said with a smile.

I responded happily, "sounds good. What do you call short? I'm glad our bags have wheels...."

Pauline then started up asking about Wanda's life in Moscow, as we travelled through the city from the Airport. About 30 minutes later, after a very interesting bus ride through very busy streets we arrived at her Apartment. The traffic consisted of many vehicles' unknown to us, full of cars, the small and medium Russian built models, Russian built trucks and buses, with many new imported brands SUV style, and sedans. The bus was electric with a closed driver compartment, with a turnstile entry. No ticket avoidance here.

We noticed immediately that the Russian people did not live in houses but multi storey apartment buildings, with high security, electronically controlled entrances of heavy steel doors. A tiny 4-person lift took us to her apartment on a higher level, where we then passed through more security doors in the lift area to her padded security door which consisted of two doors one either side of a very small air lock. The apartment was small, about the size of less than half a western style house. We stayed with her in her apartment, which was quite comfortable, after enjoying time together talking about out trip and the necessary safety talk about the life in this huge Country.

After a simple evening meal and realising how tired we were after the trip, Pauline and I slept very well. After breakfast the next day, Wanda walked us to the Railway Station, a rather long walk, to board our train for the trip to our destination. We were glad that Wanda knew her way around, as we trundled through narrow streets wheeling our suitcases along behind us, also carrying small backpacks. So, after a half hour walk through these unfamiliar streets, past small buildings of interesting stone and concrete structures, we arrived at a huge Railway Station.

The city, by their map, is 45kms by 35kms, with a number of small cities joined outside the ring like small arms. There is a loop road of 8 lanes each way, circling the city 109kms long. The population officially is 14 million but estimated at 21 million. To compare, Melbourne central (only) is 68kms by 35kms, which includes a large area of standard housing, with the total area of Melbourne population at just under 5 million. Moscow's population then, as we became aware, resides almost totally in multi storey apartment blocks, one of which we saw was 30 odd storeys high.

The transport system in Moscow is amazing, with four types; above ground trains service cities outside of this City, of which there are 5, trams, buses, and the world-renowned underground system which is awe inspiring. More on that later.

We were very happy that our YWAM guide assisted us to get our tickets, as there were about 15 ticket offices, with lines of people about 10 deep at each. This was common apparently, the attendants were certainly in no hurry, as this was an area where security for personal identification was paramount. Our passports were needed along with our visas to get our tickets. Of course, our seats on the train were pre booked in Australia, and we just needed to collect the tickets. At the time of the visit the exchange rate was A$1 to 28 Rubles, in 2020 it was A$1 to 42 Rubles. The prices for the tickets amazed us, as the trip to Krasnoyarsk for 2 people in 3rd sit up sleeping accommodation was $175 each for a trip of three and a half days, equal to a Sydney to Perth trip distance for over $2000. 2nd class was about double at $350 each and first class sleeping double again, still much cheaper in Russia. We would have been very happy to travel 1st Class. The distance to Krasnoyarsk from Moscow, is about 400km longer than the Sydney to Perth train.

The railway station was quite large with about 5 or more concrete, ground level platforms, with three trains stationary at each, our train being about 25 passenger cars. It was an open station with a long walk to our carriage, which was attended by two Russian women, one of whom was quite solidly built. They spoke English sufficiently enough to be understood. We were directed to our doorless compartment halfway along the side corridor, consisting of 6 bunks, a stack of three on each side of a central table, the top two being for blanket storage, and one set of two in the passage. We were soon to learn that we were sharing with four young African females, which of course was not at all appropriate, so we all agreed that, as I was allocated an upper bunk, Pauline and I would use the passage bunks and table, and they could have the compartment. There was no way I could climb into an upper bunk, much too high, and me not being nimble enough to climb ladders.

We settled into the trip but were able to only relate to a few people of different nationalities due to a lack of language. The African girls all were English speaking and easy to converse with on a friendly level, but we left them to their own company and didn't bother them, apart from the occasional chit chat. The train trip was a very interesting experience, as we flew through huge pine and birch forests, miscellaneous towns and villages, on the main rail artery of Russia from west to east. Meals needed to be purchased from Railway towns along the way on the platform from private vendors. On board we were given a glass cup with a metal holder, as there are hot water boilers by the Attendants office for hot tea and coffee drinking. At night I would sit up and stare out into the darkness as we glided through those dark towns basically lit, with large railway yards showing up alongside of this main line.

Passenger changes were few, and at one stop a Chinese or Mongolian woman and 3 children came on board, and the African girls left the train there. Once they settled, I noticed that she was reading a bible to her children, so we made contact with her, and each shared our faith. She was actually teaching her children from the Bible during the remaining trip to her destination.

I relate now an amusing situation where, on our last morning, I wanted to spoil Pauline for breakfast, so I walked through the train to the first-class carriage dining room kitchen. With a total language barrier, I ordered a meal by sign language, which I paid for. What I did not realise was that we then stopped at a large Station. "Oh darn, what now?"

Once again, using sign language, the waitress followed me towards the back of the train, and she stepped out onto the platform with my meal on a tray held high. She looked at me questioningly as I indicated for her to follow me as we needed to step back into my carriage. She did follow me pushing through the train load of passengers now having alighted from the train. I felt quite embarrassed now, doing this, it must have looked quite strange with the waitress holding the tray of food above her head as we did so, into my carriage 3 cars from the dining room. We both ascended the steps into the carriage to Pauline's and my section where she gave the meal to her. I really felt for the waitress, so I thought I had better tip her.

She gave me a big smile as I introduced her to Pauline who then blushed at the thought of the trouble taken by the waitress.

"Oh Graham, you shouldn't have…"

"Oh yes I should…." Sitting down to gloat at the strange looking Russian breakfast in front of her.

My walk through the carriages to the dining car, showed me the vast variety of nationalities, many with Chinese of Mongolian features, with a large number of Russian men and women, who traditionally were of big and or strong build. Some of them eyed me with suspicion, especially when I walked through with my movie camera on my right shoulder filming the scene, as inconspicuously as possible. The scenes were of a very busy train of people packed in like sardines lounging about in various states of undress, well worth the risk of getting a movie of Russian transport and the lives of these people.

Our objective, on the train, was to observe and film as much of the trip as possible, regarding the scenery, towns and villages, and the railway system, which was electric. The main point observed was that we were made aware that this railway line is the lifeblood of Russia crossing the country from west to east, so with so many railway crossings en-route no collision with vehicles could occur. Therefore, all railway crossings were manned and secured by popup steel plates on the roadway which prevented any vehicle from crossing the tracks when a train approached.

Krasnoyarsk

After those three and a half days, we arrived at Krasnoyarsk to be met by Garry and Christie at the railway station for our 8-week stay with them and the family. Garry had his own SUV 4-wheel drive, and so after a short trip, we arrived at a very large suburb of many 10 storey apartment blocks spread out over the area with gardens and car parks surrounding them. They had a generous apartment on the third floor of a 10-storey block in the central area of the city at a large intersection of roads and a supermarket within easy walking distance. It was a spacious 3 bed area, almost open plan entrance hall, kitchen, and lounge, well furnished. Christie had organised to feed us all, including their 3 children, which rather choked the kitchen with people. It was a happy time of chatting and eating as we had not met with them for over 6 months. They then drove us to our own apartment on the other side of the city, which was divided by a deep gully and large traffic roundabout.

The roads are wide, with large centre traffic islands, side gardens and wide paths. Areas between the buildings have gardens with narrow service roads jammed with parked cars. There are no personal car garages, only a large dirt allotment where parking is allowed for a fee. Garry parks his vehicle in the local car park. The traffic is horrendous, fast, with no care for the speed limit. Traffic lights are operated on a timed crossing frequency, but many drivers ignore them if they can get away with it. A Police fine for speeding is very low, about A$5.

The City is also split with a large, wide, shallow, clear water river, cold and fast flowing, on the western side of which is the business district. This river supplying the city with drinking and most water needs, hot water being supplied by two means, one being a 2m deep underground main supply, and with older apartments, a furnace in the basement supplying the hot water needs of the Apartment.

The object of our visit was to assist Garry and his team with visits to villages to assist with whatever work was needed towards evangelism and ministry to children.

12

God With Us

On one of our walks across a large traffic roundabout, there was a man wearing Army attire, sitting in a wheelchair in the centre of the island. We all walked past him, and then it hit me,

"What are we doing here, I should have stopped and prayed for that man." I verbalised that statement loudly in disgust to the group, raising my arms in the air. On the way back I did just that, getting a very warm reception from him, as he accepted my attention to him. This happened occasionally as we travelled around.

Another incident where the Lord had us minister, was at the old original Airport terminal, where Pauline wanted to look around a Market nearby. I wasn't interested in the Market, so I noticed, in my wandering among the many people there, a beggar sitting on a cardboard mat on the steps in front of the Airport building. I retrieved Pauline, and we went to speak to the man.

Once we had his attention, he looked at us and he appeared to be blind, but it may have been cataracts as he seemed to see us. We laid hands on him, and then he lifted his arms, and we saw what could have been self-mutilation, we were shocked to see that he had no hands. They had been cut off from the wrists. We wept for him as I took hold of his head and spoke out in power in the Holy Spirit as I knelt beside him and then hugged him.

It wasn't long before Garry arrived to collect us in his SUV, so we left the man in God's hands. I looked around to where we spoke to him and he was gone, cardboard seat and all. God is in control.

I could relate more of the Russian environment and travel; however, this is not a travel guide but my testimony of how my family is led by God in our lives in His love and grace. There are many more events to follow. What we found in this Siberian city was that there are only two forms of living accommodation: the old established timber homes of some size, on quarter acre self-sustaining blocks of land, and 10 story concrete, very secure, apartment blocks. We were housed in one of these very small apartments, which was owned by the pastor of one local Lutheran church who was on a trip to the USA. His mother had been the occupant, but had been placed in a nursing home, so we were able to have this apartment leased to us. A one room 'L' shaped bedroom come lounge, one small kitchen with a small table and two stools, and a heated bathroom. The 'L' shaped room had one single bed and one 2-person lounge chair. The stove had only one working element, but it was just ok to cook a meal. We were actually happy to experience how the Russian people lived, which gave us an appreciation of their lifestyles. This apartment block, being one of many probably built over 50 years ago in the Communist era, where security was over the top, had 4 key-locked doors to open to get into our apartment.

Once we were settled in, we set about working with Garry and his team visiting several villages within a few hours' drive of the City, to not only mix with the people, but carry out repair or building work to their homes. A main feature of working with the basic living standard of the local people, was also the way work was carried out and this included their style of faith and worship. Evangelism was a key with Garry and the team carrying out programs with village children and their families. He was assisted by a young Russian couple as part of his team, which was essential until Garry and his family learnt the Russian Cyrillic language. The woman, 'Anya', was also our interpreter.

I was given the opportunity to Minister in a few local Churches of different denominations or groups. This was a new experience for me which did produce some results. We found that the people were very friendly and there was an expectation from them for us, as westerners, to assist them or help them in some way. They were very hospitable.

Part of the ministry in visiting the villages, through contacts in the Christian churches there, was to encourage the people in their faith. As I mentioned earlier, Garry had this personality where he could easily mix with the people there and befriend them, so we had an invite to a house where they were having a musical evening with praise and worship songs, a meal and fellowship. I had noticed that part of the group were obvious weightlifters and quite fit young men, muscular, so after the music session an arm-wrestling competition started. Two men stood out from the crowd, one was a short stocky human 'A' frame, and the other a huge 6'4" man of some hulk. Garry and I, as I found to my dismay later in another trip, were both overweight, but Garry was quite strong and competed with the short guy and lost, of course. The competition went on, and considering I was also reasonably fit due to my earlier job of waste removal, I challenged a young man of about 35 years, who was quite muscular to a wrestle.

He shook his head and waved me away, "No, you too old."

I laughed and beckoned him to the table, "Come on here," as I grinned at him.

Now I was taking a risk here, but I was not necessarily a stranger to arm wrestling, but I understood the young guy's hesitancy as I was obese. So, we took our seats opposite each other, elbows together, hands gripped, eye to eye.

He tested me, by flexing his arm against mine, his eyes widened as I did not flinch,

"Oh," and he smiled.

He was strong, Garry, to his amusement, said, "Graham, you're mad...."

Someone said, "Go...", and we strained against each other, and I realised there was no way I could put him down, so I decided I would hold him as best I could. I strained and held as hard as I could for about 2 minutes, until my upper arm felt as if either my muscles would tear or my arm break, due to the pain, so I dropped my arm back.

There was a cheer in the room, as I sat back exhausted, and the young man and I looked at each other. We both stood up as he gave me a big grin of approval and we had this massive hug together. This was an experience I will never forget.

To top it off, almost every home has a 'Banya', and this home had one, smaller than most, fitting about two people. It is a Russian adaptation of a 'Sauna', and these 'Saunas' are very hot, about 80 deg C. Remember our parent's generation had their 'copper' of boiling water with a fire underneath, well the 'Banya' has a 44-gallon drum with a large fire underneath. Talk about sweat, in fact with this one, I had to leave the door open to get some air. The head is throbbing, and the feet are cold. They have wooden benches to lie on for an even sweat. 20 minutes is all I could handle.

Such is the wonder of living and ministering in Russia, a beautiful Country. We went back to Russia twice more, once in 2012 to Krasnoyarsk with Garry and family, and in 2013 we went to Moscow to work with Ebenezer Fund International, working with the Jewish people living there to encourage them to perform 'Aliyah' in returning to Israel according to Scripture. More of this trip later.

Camping

Our second trip to Krasnoyarsk, to visit Garry and Christie, started as a bit of a laugh as we went camping before we took off up north with a team. Camping in Russia is rather different than at home, so Pauline and I, with Garry and his family, went to Lake Belo south of Krasnoyarsk. We travelled there with Garry in his 4WD, Christie and the 3 kids in her small sedan, and a friend of theirs, Vadim and his family, were to come later in his Station Sedan and trailer.

The road around the main lake skirted quite large private areas of about 10 acres, all fenced, and some had quite a few campers in them, but one needed to pay money to stay there. So, we carried on past these areas to an open beach area surrounded with low saltbush type of fauna. Friends were to come later to stay with us. We set up camp just off the beach, with Garry and family in their large tent, and Pauline and I in a smaller one next door. Once set up, Garry pumped up an inflatable boat, and he and his 3 kids enjoyed a canoe ride. We enjoyed the afternoon just relaxing by the shore watching them do their thing.

The area around the lake was quite barren of forestry, with low grasses and bushes, being sparse, with high hills some distance away on the other side.

An evening meal organised by Christie, was well received and filling, so after some topical conversation, we retired.

A drive around the lake the next morning to the distant hills was rewarding, as we were able to walk up a steep grassy slope to a ridge to take in a glorious view of the whole area. Back to the camp for lunch, with Vadim and his family arriving shortly after. Garry drove into the area in a 4wd, but Vadim had his station wagon and trailer, and got bogged in the soft earth.

Now the fun started. A rainstorm with dark black clouds came rapidly from the east, so we all, apart from Vadim and Co, crammed into Garry's tent, huddled together out of the heavy downpour. This was very unexpected as the sky had been quite clear so far. The storm lasted for about 40 minutes and then cleared and so we ventured out to take in the very wet area around our tents. Vadim did not fare too well, so we all got together to un-bog his car and trailer. He hadn't even had time to pitch his tent.

The fun continued, a couple of hours later that rainstorm turned around and came back to haunt us, so back into the tent, to wait it out. More torrential rain.

Above the camp area we dug a small pit with a toilet tent erected over it. For everybody's use. During the quiet between the two downpours, I dug a new toilet, that was a waste of time, as the storm gave us a self-flushing toilet to cope with. It was full of water.

After a group discussion, we realised that our little camping trip was over as the slope to the water became a bog. The decision made, we stayed overnight and packed up the next morning to drive out.

Two Russian families set up camp the same day we arrived, about 50 meters away, so we went to mingle with them for a short while. I yelled out to Garry, "Hey do you see what they have done over there."

"Yeah, I think they have made themselves a 'Banya'." A sweat box.... They certainly had. They dug a hole in the coarse sand, climbed into it and pulled a tent cover over their heads. I don't know how they heated it, but when we got there one of the men said: "Hey, come and join us, plenty of room in here....", No there wasn't.

They were laughing, and enjoying themselves, wearing shorts covered in dirt, with an air of vodka intoxication. We laughed with them. Garry practised his Russian language on the men as we enjoyed their company for what it was, and then we retired for our evening meal, Christie having shown her skills along with Garry's assistance.

The next day showed us that the Russian roads are not really roads but tracks and mud bogs. The road in from the main road was a somewhat trenched two-wheel track, built especially for those drivers with 4wd skills, but now full of water. Once we came to the main inroad to the area, this was real mud. A road about 20m wide with water filled potholes and trenches on each side, and oh! It was uphill. Christie, in her small two-wheel-drive car seemed to slither forward slowly, with Garry wandering from side to side through the potholes. Occasionally a car would slither past us in the opposite direction, having us heading for a trench, but finally, after getting our footwear filled with mud helping Christie's bogged car, we arrived at the main bitumen road where we stopped to clean up.

Garry warned us regarding Russian road rules, "We need to make sure that our number plates are clean, otherwise if stopped by the Police, we'll get a fine."

We then washed the cars and our shoes with what water we had and continued on the long drive back to Krasnoyarsk. Plenty of joyful conversation took place on a disastrous camping holiday by a popular lake 'Resort'.

"Well Garry, that was a real experience mate." As I laughed aloud, "Never been on a camping trip like that before."

"You should be here during the in season, the place is chockers. This lake area and two others, plus Baikal are the only freshwater lakes in Asia of note."

"True I guess, the walk up the hill was a bonus, the whole area was a refreshing experience and what a diverse landscape. Loved it." The camping holiday over, back to the reason for the season.

Mission Trip

The plan was for a trip with a team to the north of Siberia, to the village of Tokuchet, north of Krasnoyarsk, for a work assist program for the village. Christie and the children didn't go, but 4 YWAM girls joined Pauline, Garry, and I for the trip there. Our interpreter and YWAM girl Anya, and her husband Zhenya, came as well in their car.

It involved a full day trip to the town near the Arctic circle on the banks of the river Chuna. We were on an invite for a work detail with an American mission family, who had been given a plot of land and a house by the village elders. He was building an underground hot house powered by internal combustion of rotting flora and supported financially by his Church in the USA. It was an experimental system to support the village and others with food during the extreme winters experienced in the higher latitudes of the Country.

It was a rugged trip over roads where Russia has a reputation, the surfaces being varied from mainly gravel to rough bitumen, and dirt, with varying widths from a lane each way to as wide as 30m. The freezing winters determine the nature of the roads, from one year to the next.

Our lunch stop, one I would never expect, and would not want to visit again, was at a roadhouse like no other. Two buildings plus a toilet which lined an embankment at the edge of a pot holed dirt parking area 50m wide, where two trucks were parked and a few cars. Only a few people were attending the buildings which offered food. Two or three petrol pumps were close to the buildings. Now the toilet, this was a gem, it hung over the embankment, and at the bottom were the remains of processed food dropped by the inhabitants. Inside the toilet shed was a hole through which you disgorged that processed food or liquid. That was it.

This roadhouse was more isolated than that of Central Australia. We were glad to continue our journey. We turned left from the 'highway' some kilometres further on for a trip along a gravel road for 50kms before we arrived at the end of this dead-end road at our village destination. A small village of about 200 residents on the banks of a very wide, slow flowing river.

Justus, his wife, and 2 children lived in a typical Russian house, which was roomy and cosy, built of tree logs and pine offcut timber roofing over insulation. Our accommodation was dormitory style but girls in one room and men in another. It turned out that Justus' young child was ill, so an attempt was made too late to isolate her, and so the virus spread to the girls. Overnight 2 were ill, one was touched with it. As was Pauline, but Garry and I managed to get past it - sort of. It hit us very quickly, with Justus and his wife apologising for the problem. The next problem was the nits, millions of the little sods, tiny flies which bred in the impenetrable forests on the other side of the river, and they gave us little stinging bites. So, nets over the head and long sleeve shirts to be worn.

The next day Garry, Justus, and I looked around the property, about 1/3rd of an acre, with a gigantic hole covered by a metal roof about 10m above the ground, so it was a single storey and basement 'barn'. The hole was about 4m deep 35m long by 25m wide. A ramp allowed access into the hole. The ground was compacted sand and had been easily dug. Timber walls were being built, and a floor just below ground level for a separation between the underground room and the ground level barn.

My job was to build a roof over a room extension of the end of the house using the pine offcuts. Boy, talk about rough, but I did it. We were there for a week, Garry had his job working with the team on the barn, and the girls were given a job of building a fence at one of the houses in the village for a widow. Justus was amazing, as he was legally blind, he still managed to drive his tractor 25km's to a forest to collect timber for the project.

Pauline and I, at the end of a day, walked down the street to the river for a break. The water was shallow and a 'gravel bar' across the river causing damming of the water and a cascade over it. This river was always frozen during winter, and when the water thawed, ice flows dredge the river bottom causing numerous damming places. I timed the flow of the water at about 15km/h from the pond. The water was ice cold.

Once the jobs were done, we were treated by two of the village women who brought us gifts and food, and fellowship and prayer were the order of the day, with a sumptuous meal provided. The virus did not hang around for long thankfully, but it certainly hit us in guts and caused some anxiety.

With our project time gone, but with achievements recognised and appreciated by the locals, we all set off back home to Krasnoyarsk, and really nearing the end of our visit to this beautiful Country of Russia.

Just one more village to mention, which was our first, and that was the village where we stayed in the Lutheran Church building, which was a normal house. The object of this visit was to build a 'Banya' in the adjacent building which had been built over a large well. Garry organised a children's get together for teaching, and Pauline was enlisted to teach a local women's group all who were attached to the Church. This is where we learnt how the village population lived. The Banya building was just being started the day we were due to leave, as the forest men did not deliver the timber until then.

There was also a humanitarian issue here, where an elderly homeless husband and wife were conveyed with us to this home to be cared for in their old age. From memory, they were also suffering from dementia. This was authorised by the Krasnoyarsk Government through the Lutheran Church.

The village properties had mini market gardens on their ½ acre lots, but this church property did but was not utilised, even though there was a married couple who lived there. The house was heated by a typical outside furnace for circulation of hot water through a 300mm pipe fitted around the inside of the outside wall of the whole house, but the toilet was about 15m away behind the Banya shed/house, to where one does not walk in the middle of the night in -40 deg C winters.

This building was in poor condition, as the floor in the female dormitory had collapsed, and the internal infrastructure was very basic. We all managed of course. We also installed a washing machine in the kitchen area which we transported to the house from Krasnoyarsk and involved a bit of nous to get it to operate. As the water supply was from a pumped well, we mounted a large plastic container 4m up on a platform attached to the wall, and bucketed water into it, them plumbed an outlet into the washing machine to give it gravity feed water for operation. Quite innovative actually. It worked.

Due to the lack of construction of the 'Banya', and Garry and his team teaching the children and Pauline with the women, I was at a loose end. Garry and I, through this whole trip, would go for physical exercise in the form of running or walking, so in this village, in the mornings we would do this and walk the main road. Remember, we were both obese weight wise, so this was his way of cutting down on the weight. We would both walk up the hill from the village on a wide dirt road into the forest, me - just to the top of the hill and he would jog for about 10km up and back.

On the mornings when Garry was busy, I prayer walked the village, while looking out for some of the people. At the same time, I took about 35 photos of the old derelict and occupied houses, mounting 4 photos in a frame, after we arrived back home. The main walk I did was back up the hill on the main road with the object of connecting with the Lord. This I did, in the middle of Russia standing in the middle of the road, in the thick of the forest I stood arms raised and worshipped within that beauty…He really touched me that day. I felt such peace and contentment, in knowing that Pauline and I had answered His call to help Garry and Christie in their calling.

One of the women with whom Pauline had been teaching, invited us to her home for an afternoon snack. This was an interesting experience of learning the Russian ways. We walked through a large gate, to be confronted with a muddy path, and see two men slaughtering a calf, 20 feet from the front door of the house. Then we entered the lean-to entrance, removed our footwear, and were ushered into a large kitchen with a dining table. Our host, Valentina, in good jovial spirits, then offered us her home-made spirits, Vodka, just brewed perhaps, then some bacon fat, great chunks of it, (skin to flesh), and brought out a large round of freshly made cheese which was still warm and wet. Out of respect, Garry and I threw down the vodka, and then chewed on the pig fat. Nearly threw up on that one, but the cheese was very fresh and tasty. There is so much more that I can relate of our experiences in this village, being able to give glory to God for the experience of ministering to these great village people who actually are still living in a bygone era.

13

Moscow

2013, another Mission trip, this time with Ebenezer Emergency Fund International, based in Moscow. It is a Jewish organisation in conjunction with two Russian welfare organisations, the object being to supply Jewish people with medical products, finance, and food parcels for these poor living in Moscow. The focus then is to encourage these Jewish families to migrate to Israel, (called Aliyah) their spiritual home, according to prophecies in Ezekiel and other passages in God's word.

Pauline and I applied to the organisation to be part of a team in Moscow and surrounding areas, with the backing of our fellowship leaders, Jenny and Brian Hagger. We were accepted, and we then made arrangements for our Visas to return to Russia in their summer, as was the case with our previous visits.

Pauline and I were privileged to be able to serve with them. The requirement was that we serve a minimum of three-months. Although we were based in Moscow, we also spent 2-1/2 weeks in two other cities that were South of Moscow, Tombov and Koorsk. Koorsk was the city where the last Russian battle with the Germans took place in WW2.

Moscow is a vibrant city as I explained earlier, where there are also lovely park areas a short walk away from the people's apartments, where anyone can exercise their dog. We were accommodated with the Ebenezer Office Manager and our trip guide and interpreter in the manager's apartment.

Maria, a young woman in her 20s, was our guide and interpreter, who organised our home visits and visits to the Jewish association, also all tickets for the required public transport, by bus, tram train, and underground train trips. She was very quiet, and at times difficult to converse with. She was not a volunteer, but a recent employed assistant, still learning the job.

We visited thirty-six families by working with the two Jewish Mission organisations in Moscow and enjoyed 160 trips in the Moscow underground railway. A massive enterprise carrying a million people daily around the City. An incredible masterpiece of world renown, with its classic marble platform decorations, statues, and artistry. The old electric trains are fast and noisy, with a perfect timetable, as they need be, as they travel only 90 seconds apart in each direction over four levels. The map of the system is shaped as the arms of a clock and two circular routes within that area. Apart from the underground railway, public transport includes very old trams, electric buses, and medium size suburban buses. Fares are very cheap, about 11 cents a trip and always packed with people.

The families we visited were given small gifts and the medicines they ordered from the Association which was opening the door for the visits. General conversation included sharing with them our reasons for being there to offer the means of doing Aliyah, some through our interpreter/guide, and we were offered hospitality in the form of either a meal or afternoon tea. The people were always welcoming. I still would have preferred to be more hands on, especially at the Airport in Moscow assisting with luggage etc. but we never seemed to be able to get there before the Olim arrived, so we could assist them.

The visits always took considerable time out of a day due to the amount of time spent on the Metro in Moscow, so no more than two or three could be done without getting very tired. The amount of physical exercise certainly appeared to be keeping us healthy. The effort and cost of doing this job is well worth the time spent. To achieve these ends, we travelled more than 160 trips on the Metro.

Within the first day or so, after arriving in Moscow, we attended the office, and met Boris and his wife, who are the leaders of Ebenezer Russia, where we were informed about our role, and learning that the Russian Christians assisted the Jewish people in restoring the monuments that have deteriorated or been vandalised. This in turn was building reconciliation between Jews and Christians.

On one occasion, at the office, we assisted in the mailout of their monthly newsletter that goes to over 2,000 homes. This was done in the very crowded office and was a busy time with four other ladies who come in every month to do this. Lunch was massive, meat and cheese, which were provided.

We were there in Moscow for a total of eleven weeks and although it was challenging at times, it was a time that Pauline and I will never forget. We both felt hugely enriched by the whole experience and very blessed to be able to be there among these Jewish people, and of course in getting to know the Russian People and their lifestyle.

God's Presence

Although there we were limited in being able to spend quiet times and Bible reading in private, the Lord was always there to help and direct us. It took some time to get accustomed to the underground railway system, our guide trained us and, in the first week or so, this was the case. At times we were able to move around in our rest times, to travel alone in the transport system. This we enjoyed as we saw His hand assist us when we were unsure of how to navigate our way around. Occasionally we needed to change trains, and we needed to check our map and try to understand the Russian signage. This is where the Lord stepped in.

On one trip we alighted from the train and stopped on the platform to check our map where there were two choices. A tall man approached us and asked, "Excuse me can I help you?" "Oh yes, we need to get to the Smolenskaya Station, thanks."

He was about thirty-five to forty years of age, wearing colourful clothing with short trousers, sneakers, and carrying a skateboard. He pointed to the passageway off the platform, and said with a smile, "That will take you there..."

"Oh, thank you," I said, then turning to Pauline nodding to the passage.

I then turned back to thank the man again, and he was nowhere to be seen. My heart seemed warmed by his presence, as we then realised, he had to be an angel sent by our Lord. He was so out of place in that environment.

On another trip on the train, we were stuck with the same dilemma and sitting in the carriage between stations, a woman opposite was looking at us, and then approached us, asking, "Can I help you?' in good English. Pauline asked her, "What station do we get off at to go to the Palace gardens?"

"I will show you; we get off in a little while." The train stopped at about two stations on, and she alighted from the train with us and indicated where to go, she then got back on the next train to continue her journey. Now, I cannot be certain if she was an angel, but an angel inspired her to help us.

The Lord used us in many ways. On another journey on the underground, two men in military uniforms were walking through and playing a guitar and singing. One only walked with one leg on a crutch and the other appeared also to be a war veteran. They continued on and when we got to our station, we alighted and saw the men sitting on a bench on the platform, which to me appeared odd as they had been on the same train and must have been very quick to get there to the bench. I was inspired to pray for these men, so Pauline and I agreed together and approached them.

As there was a language barrier, sign language was the order of the day, so with clasped hands in prayer mode, and then pointing upwards, I indicated our desire for them. They gladly accepted and held out their hands. We prayed over them in English as they nodded in acceptance. In their eyes I saw such gratitude as tears flowed and one handshake was very strong as they replied to us in Russian. I do not think they wanted us to go.

Many of the Jewish people we visited asked us the question with emotion in their voices: "You are a surprise to us, that you come here to see us all the way from Australia, at you own expense, to visit us and tell us these things. Are you Christians?"

"Yes, we love the Lord as you do, and come in obedience to Jesus words in helping you to return to Israel, as said in the Bible, in the book of Ezekiel." The affection showed to us by these people was genuine. So, our visit and conversation surrounding Aliya for them, was accepted joyfully, as we read the appropriate verses to them when applicable.

A very encouraging piece of news came our way the next year having returned home after our trip there, when the two daughters of the Australian family representatives for Ebenezer were involved in the same ministry in Moscow. They sent us a photograph of a family Pauline and I visited, with the two young women who followed up this family. They had decided to migrate to Israel. The punch line was that they did this because: "Pauline and Graham visited us and encouraged us to make the move." I couldn't help but weep as that made that trip very worthwhile due to that result.

We went in faith that the Lord wanted us to go and weren't sure what we would be doing as volunteers but were pleasantly surprised when we were briefed as to what was expected of us. Along with our interpreter who was with us 99% of the time we were there, we visited the older Jewish Holocaust survivors to deliver to them prescribed medicine that the Jewish Association in Moscow gives to them. It was a wonderful time visiting these folk and we were hugely blessed as we sat with them and listened to their stories. They appreciated being visited by two Aussies from so far away and told us so! I felt that the verse in 2 Corinthians 'That God was in Christ reconciling the world to Himself and He has given to us the ministry of reconciliation' was our mandate.

We found them friendly and independent with a confidence and optimism about them. We were also to encourage them to go back to Israel as God was calling them back as He is also calling the Gentiles to assist in their return. This story is found in Isaiah 49 and Ezekiel 36. We discovered that many had responded and were making Aliyah, as most weeks during the months of July – September saw twenty-five persons each week at the airport heading to Israel to make it their home. It was also part of our work to assist in their transition at the airport by helping to carry their bags from the van into the check in counter. Also, we had some wonderful fellowship with the ones that spoke some English; just chatting and being with them while they waited in queue. We were amused to find that some were even taking their dogs with them to Israel!

For the first three weeks we were able to help the Olim at the Airport, but as we were away in Tambov, and Koorsk for most of July and August, airport trips did not occur again until later in the month. This time we were able to relate to some of the people waiting and Pauline was able to give up some of her gifts. But I was still very apprehensive regarding approaching any of the groups. Two Army personnel and one security guard were present, and on one visit he stood between us and the group of students. I believe that for us to be able to relate to these people we must have identification and we must be introduced by Maria or Valera (our driver) to the group as to who we are. I was even stopped from taking a photograph of the group. It was no problem in the first two visits as we helped the Olim into the airport building with their luggage, and so introductions were already there, but I.D. was still necessary. But now there was no physical assistance needed as they were already inside. Even Maria has no badging as does the Jewish association Rep. I believe this should have been essential.

Our first trip to the airport was an eye opener, as the main highway travelling south of Moscow went straight to the airport and stopped there at a massive traffic jam, which had nowhere to go, even the car park was too small. The Interior of the building was massive, 60 check in points with hundreds of people lined up doing their thing. The Jewish check ins were a different check in system totally and at the quiet end of the terminal. This is where the security men tended to be continually present while Maria did the paper work for the incoming Jewish families.

We met our first family outside on the service road in a vehicle there where a mother, with her married daughter and her husband, were unloading their goods and valuables for the trip to Israel. We helped them in with her bags - about six big stripey type – and then we chatted for quite some time on and off as we were very early. The plane was not due to take off till around midday. It was hard for Pauline, as she became very choked up realizing the importance of it all, and it also being our first experience of Olim returning. The married daughter seemed very young, about twenty or possibly younger, but she may have been older. They were going to Israel because they had been thinking about it for a long time. Her other daughter lives in Israel with her husband and daughter and they will all be living fairly close to each other. The mother was very impressed with the title of the organization, Ebenezer, meaning 'stone of help' which she explained comes from the Psalms of David as she put it. She was intending to do more study on the word. She felt that it had a much deeper meaning. This struck a chord with us. I think that she has had a rhema word from the Lord. Pauline was intending to do some study herself on 'Ebenezer', 'stone of help'.

During our time in Moscow, we sometimes went to the ICF (International Christian Fellowship) Church on Sunday. We introduced ourselves to one Pastor in July, but this month we were there late, and only were able to speak to some Russians there after the service.

In the cities of Tambov and Koorsk we were greeted like people from Mars, and highly respected as we shared about ourselves and the Ministry, this occurred about six times. We were really feted, especially since we came 'all the way' from Australia, at our expense. We were truly humbled by their love towards us.

Tombov

The journey to Tombov was a day's train trip, and was worth the effort, especially in sharing in the Churches, which did not happen in Moscow. We were welcomed by Tatiana, our Local representative and guide/interpreter, along with Boris and Valentina. They were excellent company, and very talented in their commitment, so we enjoyed this City very much. Tombov was a beautiful city, with massive gardens along the banks of this botanically tree lined and lawned river gliding past the city. There were many people walking to and fro along cement paths, enjoying the solace and taking in the scents of the flowers. Trees and flower beds lined the major thoroughfares of the city which was a picture of nature's splendour.

After being showed our accommodation we settled into getting to know the area. Our sleeping quarters were in the top mezzanine floor of a large cathedral size church building. As a result of being there in the church, we attended a Sunday meeting with the people, which was very inspiring as to the form of the service, not unlike our own large churches.

Tatiana had a program of church visitation and speaking engagements planned for the first weekend, and a service both Thursday and Friday nights in two different places. Our first engagement was on Sunday morning at the Pentecostal Church on the city fringe where Pauline shared about the Ebenezer Fund Mission. The Pastor and his wife and two elders shared a meal with us after the service honouring us by which we were greatly blessed. All of the visits here were quite different in their spirituality and the people very appreciative and loving to us for our attendance. In Tatiana's Church I was asked to share my testimony to a large group, which was daunting but very well received.

We attended another church service elsewhere of about fifty persons where there was male and female segregation which I thought was strange. Regardless, Pauline and I were very impressed with the commitment of the people and their leaders during the service to worship. It appeared that it was a special service, as here was an Armenian Pastor and one of his elders as guest speakers there, Pauline and I, as guests, and we were also asked to share.

I believe that the meeting was in English for us and maybe other guests as well to understand. The leaders I know, did, as I recall, understand the form of service, which was very different. Three times a different leader led in prayer, preached, then led worship. When the music started the mainly female congregation threw their hands up over their heads and made rowdy worship. During this meeting I was asked to share, and needing encouragement, I grabbed Pauline's hand, moved to the front of the meeting and shared my personal testimony. The Armenian pastor was reasonably vocal, saying 'Amen, Amen', and I could see in his face how he was almost overcome at hearing what I had to say. The leader, who led the last of the trilogy, came up to us after the meeting and thanked us for sharing and then said, "You must love your wife very much, I have rarely seen a husband and wife holding hands." His face showed his surprise at perhaps an uncommon thing in Russia.

The meeting did not end there. Their commitment showed another aspect of this body of Christ, as the congregation was divided into two groups, the women downstairs and the men upstairs. We were invited to participate in a foot washing ceremony, every person washed the other participants feet in rotation. It was very well organised, and I was quite overcome as a visitor, to be honoured in this way, along with the other men.

Pauline and I and our team had earlier been invited to another church meeting and I was asked to share around the word, a new experience for me as it was only the second time, apart from a meeting in Krasnoyarsk. It was a small church of about thirty people, and I shared something of my Christian experience as an encouragement to them in their walk. After I shared, I was inspired by the Holy Spirit to prophesy over a teenager who was part of the Worship music group. It was in essence, "God has anointed you with the gift of music, a skill you are blessed with to bring the people to worship Him, so as you grow in stature, your skill will mature as you come before me." I must say his skill was a blessing in the meeting as we worshipped. This meeting went one step further, as I was so humbled, I was stuck for words after the meeting, when the congregation left, but our two guides, with the elders, Pauline, and I were taken into a back room where we all joined together for a sumptuous meal. Pauline and I looked at each other, and I was really embarrassed as I realised, we were being treated as visiting overseas speakers of importance. As I said I was stuck for words realising that! I thought, "Is the Pastor expecting me to give the team words of wisdom and encouragement during the meal?" I had no idea what to say, I had no experience with this type of appreciation and honour, I was so humbled.

During our stay in the city, we were invited to another church meeting, and once again feted with being part of a Passover meal, which was very moving. About ten to twelve people crowded into a small narrow room around a long table. Pauline and I had only ever been part of this celebration once before in the past in our own Church home fellowship honouring the Jewish feast. It was a pleasure and very meaningful to be part of this family meal with Russian people. Later in the evening we walked back to our host church for a well-earned rest from the events of the following days. One of the women who was very hospitable, walked back to the church with us and we found it all locked up. The conversation was joyful during the long wait there, until we were met at the gate by the caretaker lady, who scolded us for being so late, "Where have you been, it is so late, I was in bed asleep and I was woken by you, you must come early, I close gates..." We apologized, not really being aware of that, after all it was only about 11.30pm.

Once our visit here was over, Boris, our musician friend drove us to Koorsk, west of Tombov, to our next accommodation. Just Pauline, our national guide and me. I must mention here that, as an old driving instructor, I was rather concerned at his driving habit of coasting down hills in neutral gear, which is actually dangerous in relying on the vehicle's brakes, so, I asked him, "Hey Boris, back in Australia I was a driving instructor, and I am concerned that you run down the hills out of gear, why?" The car was small, cramped, and uncomfortable, the Russian national home-made cheapy. He said defensively, "I save petrol, it's OK, we are safe...." We made it......

Koorsk

Koorsk was very different, a large city, where there was a very wide avenue about 4kms long, dedicated to the second world war with old military hardware placed in the centre gardens of the road. A huge war memorial had been built at the high end of the road with all the names of the war heroes and the dead inscribed on the granite walls inside the building. It was magnificent and could be seen for miles. The Military hardware, old mobile heavy calibre guns, a tank, and many others were able to be seen. The curvature of the road from top to bottom gave a splendid view of the whole avenue, a sight to behold. Our impressions of Russian cities were that they showed a huge pride in their dedication honouring their war heroes and victories. Huge statues of Lenin also were noted in every city to honour his efforts to build up the Russian Empire. Their buildings also endeared this attitude of National pride and Glory from their splendour.

Boris, was our main guide and Valentina, our local guide, along with Marsha (Maria) our interpreter. Having been met by her we were shown around the main central area of Koorsk and then taken to our billet.

Once again, we were accommodated on a church property of some size, in an outbuilding. The property was on a main road with a tram line along one side. From memory, while walking along that line, I could have dropped my phone, as I was not able to find it later. No more phone. The day after our arrival was Sunday and we were invited, and escorted by Valentina, to a Pentecostal church service where we were to share the vision and our personal testimony.

Before the meeting, we met with a Jewish family living opposite the church who gave us a meal, and the woman asked us again after the service for another meal. Huge amounts of very different food, Russian of course, was consumed, some of it anyway, and very well received, after which we prayed a blessing over the family. Meeting with this family and spending time with them in their house was a huge blessing to us, it was obvious that they went to much effort in providing for us, realising that their means may have had them on the borderline of being able to provide. We had a great time of singing and I even danced to a spectacular tune, played, and written by our guitar playing Russian host. I felt a very strong anointing to dance, something I had never done in worshipping our Lord.

There is always more to these stories, as you would expect, with the time of fellowship with this Jewish family and the church family opposite.

What we had to say in the service was well received. The church was packed full to overflowing which showed to us that Christianity was certainly not dead in Russia. After the service while we were all seating around the room chatting to the people with a cuppa and cake, there was an incident which tended to spoil our church visit. Pauline had her phone stolen from her bag sitting on the floor by her side, by a young boy who ran off. We mentioned this to the church staff once Pauline realised what had happened, but they did not show any understanding or interest in the matter.

By the end of August, we had completed over thirty-five visits to Jewish holocaust survivor's apartments, seeing that the variety of living standards and health has been high, with the very poor appearing to be very well able to support themselves. Their stories were basically the same regarding the war, most of them came from the Ukraine, and they almost all had business success stories through their high intelligence and work ethic. Only a few considered emigrating to Israel, most could not go for different reasons.

14

Police Resignation

In 1980, I was stationed at the Darlington Police Station, which was some time after we settled in the city and I had been in several posts within the department offices including records in the city HQ, scientific section, containing photography, and then back on the road in the breath analysis section for a year. I then transferred to the Darlington Police Station back on mobile patrols and then the enquiry section, finally ending up in the public office.

More and more I was becoming aware of my increasing limitations and wisdom in my applications to the tasks. One positive was in applying for the breath analysis course, where we would learn the scientific reasons for being able to conduct the tests on the analysis machine. This was the only time we were permitted to consume alcohol on duty, even to the point of moderate intoxication, how else could we test our skills and know how to test the public when on duty, if not to test each other on the course. I passed the course and was then posted to the unit. The course consisted of 10 personnel. It was for 2 weeks and was an enjoyable time actually as it was very relaxed, and we all mixed well.

This attachment went well for 8 months, once completing the course, and working from headquarters, we had our own Mitsubishi sedan car which had a metal frame to hold the testing machine between the rear seats for rear seat operation. I hated the handling of the ampoules of acid where we needed to break off the top. My end in this job came in making a serious mistake with one test due to the busyness of the moment.

I was given the radio call to attend at the Port Adelaide Police Station, where I arrived and set up the machine in a small office. A male person was seated before me, and I went through the normal procedure, and noted his BA reading at 0.15. The arresting officer then took the man from the office on completion, and immediately two officers came into the room with a rowdy customer and put him in the chair. This man was quite drunk.

I went through the usual procedure with this man and obtained a reading of 0.34. At this point whenever a person has a reading above 0.3, a blood test is required at a Hospital to verify his reading. The arresting constables therefore removed him, and he was taken to the Queen Elizabeth Hospital. I then continued with my shift.

I soon realised once they left, that in clearing the machine for this test, the machine was not totally cleared and so I had failed to clear the machine for the first test after the initial test was done. The reading was so high the offender needed to be taken to hospital for a blood test to verify my test. His actual reading was 0.19. So, the blood test showed his real reading, which, when the machine clearance result was gained, were the same. As a result, once the report hit the Sergeant's desk, I was immediately transferred as I could no longer conduct the tests, due to prosecution problems where my evidence would be questioned as unreliable. Another step towards the inevitable.

Every year the officer in charge of the station would submit a report on the member's ability and behaviour. Apparently, my behaviour was dropping, through boredom perhaps, but also over a few incidents of lack of wisdom in my dealings with the public. There also was a lack of trust by the patrol members for assistance they might require from me in their record enquiries. I was not really aware of my drop in performance, so to receive a bad yearly report was quite upsetting.

One incident I recall was while on the enquiry service, which actually had me removed from that section, was a very uncooperative person whom I was to interview over a traffic matter. I actually arrested him over a scuffle in his home requiring assistance of a cruise patrol. It turned out that the arrest was unlawful over a misunderstanding of ingress into his home. The matter was resolved, but I was transferred to general office duties.

My record now in the department had me unsuitable for country policing and unsuitable for mobile patrol duties. In the office on night shift my team could not trust me. This came about where I was unable to concentrate on more than one thing at a time, I would be reading when a patrol would call me for doing routine checks and I could not hear the call. I actually had the hand radio on my shoulder alongside my ear but to no avail. This was contrary to my ability in 1975 when stationed in the police operations room that year when I had that wonderful spiritual transformation, where I was able to do several things at once quickly. At this time then, in retrospect, my abilities 10 years on had deteriorated substantially, as if in a fog. It was obvious that my time as a police member was coming to an end. I attempted to be transferred to the workshop driving team, but there no vacancies and not likely to be. I certainly did not want to commute to and from city headquarters.

You may see the effect of my deteriorating mindset, mental state and or attitudes. I certainly came to realise that myself in just writing this testimonial, where my faith was sliding caused, I believe, from a lack of commitment to the faith. This needed to change.

Pauline and I discussed our future, and realised I needed to resign, and the only solution being is that we needed to do something else. She came up with an idea when talking to friends, of a garden waste removal business. So, we made our enquiries and decided it may be something worth trying.

A Witness of Bible Numerics

As a new believer, in 1975, I read a book called 'The Power of Positive Thinking' by Norman Vincent Peale 1952. I had always been a negative thinker, and so in reading this book it changed my attitude towards eliminating negative language and mindset, which fell in line with Jesus' words in the Gospels.

Another one I had read was a 'Bible Numerics' book by Ivan Panin. There are many other books covering the subject, but Ivan's book was very straight forward and worth reading. It sets out the discovery of the numerical system in the Hebrew language, as associated by the Bible writings, which proves beyond doubt that the book is divinely inspired by God, as no man could write it but by divine inspiration.

Then, having acknowledged the above faults in me, and to use the Christian wording, sin, which means disobedience, I changed my outlook with the help of our Lord Jesus Christ. My attitudes and old self changed, so a new life and walk became so different, to read that book as a result of a recommendation, actually opened my eyes to the Lord's divinity. I was so impressed, that the negative conversations and comments disappeared as a conscious decision to be positive in that area. It all became complimentary and uplifting and so relationships blossomed in conversation. I had become a nuisance sometimes by taking the English language literally by making a joke of it which was more of an annoyance. For example, the Australian slang version of our language in phraseology changes the meaning of the expression used.

For Example: 'How ya going today?", Is very prevalent. I respond, "Oh I'm walking today...". Or "I'm driving today." Blank looks from the recipient shows total surprise at my crass humour.

"What in hell is he talking about, I tried to be nice...." perhaps this thought pervaded. Some did get the joke but only by a smile, when the comment is meant to be a question as to your health.

Therefore, within the workforce this did not appear to be well accepted and was difficult to maintain those positive attributes.

As you may now be aware, the events surrounding my employment were adding up, causing obvious mental attitudes and inabilities, not that I was aware of at that time. I often wonder what could have happened to me towards my future had not God tapped me on the shoulder.

The Big Day

The time came when on nightshift at Darlington in 1985, I was contemplating my career in the Police Department, and I was actually reading my Bible at the desk in the internal office where I was the shift supervisor, so I did what I had been taught not to do, and that is to open the book to a random page and jab the page with one finger and read what it says.

I read what it said.....'Make haste, get out of Jerusalem quickly, because they will not accept your testimony about me....." Acts 22.18. I took Jerusalem as being the police department. A short prayer was said, and within half an hour my resignation was typed and handed in to the Superintendent's 'in' basket. I started shaking at the thought of what I had just done. During my contemplation, I realised that I had completed 21 years in the police department. The number 21 in the Hebrew numerical system means maturity or adulthood as to your age. To resign from the department, I needed to give 14 days' notice. The date when I typed the resignation was 14 days before my last day of service, 7/8/1985. The number 7 is perfection, the number 8 is new beginnings, and 5 is grace. So, my first day of freedom from the department was 8/8/85, the 3 being the trinity and the 3 8's being Jesus name in the Hebrew system. So, I felt that my resignation was approved by God as a new beginning.

On that day, God spoke to me most directly proving his divine direction using the numerical system in the dates. My confidence was uplifted as being the right time to leave the police service and start a new direction. This actually goes further. Our son Adrian was born on 8/7/66, our daughter Jolie 14/7/70, and Kylie 21/5/78. The number 6 is the number for man. They all fit. It goes further again. I bought a Dodge truck for $3700, my superannuation paid back to me on resignation was $18,000, 3 6's. When I advertised by letter box drop to start the business, I received 5% return on customers, where the industry only gets about 3%. As the business grew, we eventually had 700-odd customers. So, there is a picture painted in these numbers, to indicate God's grace over the decisions made. Our God reigns!

I was on night shift when I submitted my paperwork; when I arrived home that morning at 7.30am, I failed to mention to Pauline what I had done, as I went straight to bed. Later that day, when I awoke, she told me that the boss had phoned her asking what her response may have been, she was shocked at the news and rather annoyed at me for not telling her. It was not necessarily a problem between us, as we had already planned it. It was just the timing. As it happened, the officer in charge indicated he understood God's leading in my resignation, as he was a 'believer'. It was an interesting conversation I had with him, but it was accepted, and the date of my last day was as stated before.

For the next 5 months I worked in preparing for the operation of our new occupation of garden waste removal, a wool bale in a metal frame, to be placed on a customer's property somewhere for use of removing tree pruning's, lawn clippings etc. In the current era, green council bins are used for that purpose. The truck already had a bin on the rear, so I rebuilt it to suit my purpose with a hydraulic hoist on the left side to lift the bales over the top to be emptied into the bin. Once that was done, and I had built my customer base with advertising and deliveries of the frames and bales, I was able to start the business. Pauline and I developed an accounting system by printing out accounts from a database, to be able to bill the customers. It all started in the heat of summer 1986, until 1997. I actually spent 12 years working the business, that number being perfect government.

15

The Enemy Attacks

John 10:10, "He, (the thief,) who comes to take away my sheep, comes only to kill them, He comes only to destroy. I have come so that they can live." (Easy English). Other Bible writings use some different words, but the context is the same. Mankind was created by God for His purposes. But there was a war in the heavenlies, and the evil Angel who created it was cast down to this planet and now plays havoc with us, but under God's control. So, God loves us, his creation, and after placing us here, is allowing that angel, whom we won't name, to test us with the object of calling on God's name for our test of faith in Him. This is a simplification of the whole story of course.

I want to point out the events in my life where that is true, whether Christian or not, in the way our lives run the course. The first event I mentioned in the chapter 1, the fence wire across the throat. It could have had serious results. That enemy is shrewd and uses every means to keep us away from Glory. He hates God's creation.

The main events were once I obtained my driver's licence. The first thing I did was buy a bomb of a car, with my life savings, a whole $100. (which my parents supplied anyway), which was a 1936 Morris 840 tourer. I would usually drive the car with the canvas roof back to soak up the cool breeze with the sun on my head. Much fun.

While at the Anglican Church, I met up with a very attractive Dutch girl who lived on the old Norton Summit Road. I visited her a few times and would park the car just off the narrow road in a parking bay. There was a creek on the other side of the road which had cut a deep channel, so to leave her house I needed to make a 'U' turn, in doing so, I stopped with the front wheels in the gutter, would put the car into reverse gear, reverse back and drive away. I watched a car pass behind me, a Vanguard Spacemaster. I then gunned the engine to reverse back, but instead of putting the gears into reverse, due to the distraction, I went forward nosediving into the creek. Absolute panic set in, but the event was in slow motion as I watched it happen. The car stopped dead, nose in, the driver's door flew open, (Hinges on the front of the door,) and I fell out of the car, landing on a bed of rocks, the creek water flowing over me. I sat there looking up at the car, engine revving, in fear that it would fall on me, ending my life. The miracle of this event was that the car was a convertible, and the front bar of the canvas roof flew forward and hit the steering wheel. Had I stayed in the car I would have been killed. But I wasn't. The detail of this event has stuck with me all my life, the seriousness of it being seared into my memory. What I cannot recall is how I got out of that creek. My girlfriend was standing on the other side of the road, and as I walked over to her, "What happened? I was afraid, one minute you were there, and then you were not." She said, with concern, in her quiet Dutch accent. All we could see was the rear bumper bar of the car, such was the depth of the creek below the road. The car was a write-off.

The next event was a rollover with my next vehicle, a 1948 Austin 8 convertible. With another female friend in the front seat with me, on return from a drive south of Adelaide, we rounded the bend in South Road at the Mitsubishi plant (then) at St Mary's, after a rain event, where the wheel marks were dry, but the road was wet. I steered around the corner at a reasonable speed but understeered so that the right-side wheels were on the wet. The car slid sideways onto the wet and flipped landing back on its wheels. At this time, I don't recall if the girl was injured, but she may have also gone to the Adelaide Hospital by ambulance, as I did. I still recall having a nurse pick pieces of windscreen glass from my head. Once again, a survival story. God is in control.

You may be aware that in the fifties and sixties, there were no such things as seatbelts, so these above-mentioned incidences were very serious.

In our late teenage years, my mates and I would usually be part of the party scene on weekends, and get intoxicated regularly, at private parties or Hotels. I was getting a real liking to drinking Southern Comfort whiskey in a hip flask., and the usual round of pints at the pub. So, drunk crazily driving, was the order of the day. Police car patrols were rarely seen, so there were no repercussions.

My next car was an FJ Holden 1955 sedan. My first car bought from a car dealer. It was an ex-business car, of low mileage and in excellent condition. And no, I did not write this one off, close though. I was working now but still needed a hire purchase agreement, for the low price of $1500. I was its first private owner. I make a point that I would drive this car almost every weekend while intoxicated.

I am mentioning this event to indicate my very reckless driving habits, I was actually a Hoon driver by today's standards. I would always drive to the limit with passengers on board as well. This particular weekend we were at a party at a house in Brighton, and I was being a fool by being the stage songster, paralytic drunk. We left the party; there were 4 of us and we decided to go to Victor Harbour, a distance of 97km from the city. (We were about 25km from the city). The road was the original two-lane road including Willunga Hill all the way to Victor. From Brighton, I drove to our destination at maximum speed in 45 minutes for the 70km's. This happened after midnight and the road was void of other traffic, thankfully. I was crazy, and very drunk, as were my passengers who were egging me on. As there were no seat belts in cars then any rollover would have been fatal.

One event was a real attack. We had been established in the Bethesda Church for some time, and a middle-aged woman joined the Church and latched onto Pauline and I. She went one step further, and as I was working in the police operations room; she would call when I was on night shift and bring me a pizza or other sustenance. Somehow, I saw an attractiveness about her, so I was tempted into a relationship. This could have happened, but God's word says that he always provides a way out, so He provided it. On a Sunday night service at Bethesda, once again Pauline and I, with a Pastor, were talking and this woman came into our space, and so I blurted it out about her wanting a relationship with me. Well, that was almost a scene, but the woman was shocked that I rejected her advances and made it public. The next night, Pauline and I had retired and were sleeping, when I was woken at about 1am, and I was being strangled, I opened my eyes and I saw a silver spoon in front of me, and also a very dark black shadow staring at me. All I could think of was to call on the Lord, and I gasped and yelled in my spiritual language, which caused my problem to disappear. Pauline awoke, and yelled, "What's the matter Graham." sounding shocked at hearing me. That enemy, that evil influence, used the sheet, which was tight around my neck, the spoon was the luminous hands of my alarm clock, and the dark shape was the window curtain. This incident proved to me he was attacking me physically, he provided me with a temptation as he must have understood a weakness in me and was very angry. Proof to me that that enemy is definitely a power to reckon with. I give God the glory for protecting us on that night, and at other times.

I will spare you the description of other events involving my driving habits even though I was involved in other collisions where I was the innocent party. I hope you understand that my life was meant to continue for a purpose, as I always survived my stupidity.

A Private Business

The rubbish removal business was good for our family financially, and as our marital home was freehold, it was easy to move to Reynella West, buy a block of land, and build another house, which we did to enhance my ability to work. It was an acre in size, on which I built a large shed at the bottom of the block to store equipment and do the work required. Pauline and I started designing and soon plans for the new house were made. Within our church membership, there were building contractors I could employ in building the house, e.g., a concreter, a carpenter, an electrician, and a plumber. I took on the rest of the job myself, door frames, and gyprocking etc. The business built my physical frame to a state of fitness, that after doing a day's work in the truck, I worked until 10pm every night on the interior, but little did I know that it added emotional tension, and also hardened my eye lenses to the point of needing spectacles. The whole job, regardless, taught me a massive amount in construction, which led to my work at YWAM some years later.

The reason for the move was that the house block at O'Halloran Hill was too small and the council would not allow me to buy the vacant block next door to use for the business. Working the business was hard work, and it took me the first year to become physically strong enough to actually handle it, so I adapted slowly. The best part of the job was forming relationships with the customers. As time went on, I was able to become personally involved where I was able to share my Christian faith with many of them, as many were already Church orientated. But then some relationships were getting too personal, so I was realising I was becoming double minded, and often mulling over some difficulties.

If you recall in my earlier chapters, I was introverted and having trouble with confrontation. This became a problem when coping with some customers and also when dealing with businesses when I needed repairs done to the vehicle. Other areas also were hard to deal with, especially with non-paying customers. Some conflicts would play on my mind and I would get quite stressed. I was not able to be forthright and bold in my dealings but would take a submissive role. This was also the case when I had mechanical breakdowns and needed to get repairs done quickly, either by myself or professional mechanics. Delays meant extra time on catchup.

Spiritually, I was falling away due to my need to concentrate on the job, even though I could still maintain a good relationship with the people, the stress of the job was starting to pull me away. Sunday was Church, and that was OK, but during the week, no bible reading and no prayer, even between Pauline and I, so my faith was dropping to a point where I was forgetting to follow Jesus' examples.

In the early days of our time at the Bethesda Church, I was one of those on the deacon teams in the late 70's and became close friends with Dean and Jeanette and their young children. Later, we all became part of a home group in the southern area at their home. The Bethesda Church grew quite quickly, and another home group started. These groups then formed a satellite Church - Bethesda South. During this period, Dean and I were prayer partners at his home, where I learnt for the first time that the felt presence of the Holy Spirit was in our midst and often spoke to us in prophesy and verse. We grew closer as friends and formed a bond which still exists today on a very casual basis.

Over the next few years, during the establishment of this southern fellowship, Dean was promoted to Pastor and was transferred to a church on the Eyre Peninsular. He returned to take over the Southern fellowship after another period of time. Our friendship continued as it was in his nature to love his people and nurture them. He was, and is, a very good, humble man. I mention this early in this testimony for understanding the support this fellowship gave me in my time of trouble.

The business continued to flourish, as I would get a few new customers, at the same time I took on contract customers owned by another 'bag' man. I was visiting about 40 customers a day, taking me only until about 3.00pm daily, and having 10 days off over Christmas.

Tree lopping come into the mix along the way, the occasional job where I may have needed to hire equipment, as with one job to bring down a tall pencil pine in a backyard and needed to cut it down in sections. A trailer-mounted hydraulic lift was needed to be hired to do the job, where I also needed to hire a dingo tractor to get into the back yard. It was an expensive job for the customer, but the tree was removed.

Another enemy attack came when I had a large job at Mitcham, to remove two large cypress pines from the front of a property, using my small reliable chainsaw. I was doing it from an extendable ladder with the appropriate harness, when, without consideration for the 20,000-volt power line, which I had not even noticed was there, I cut through a branch overhanging the street. Mistake. The branch fell on the power lines and jammed my chainsaw in the cut on the branch. Silly me went and grabbed the chainsaw to turn it off, when wham! like a sledgehammer to my right arm and shoulder, I was almost thrown from the ladder, yes, silly me went and did it again, thinking that the chainsaw was insulated by the rubber mountings.... not so. I went into a state of shock, almost losing consciousness.

The homeowner called the power company, who came and shut down the power so I could remove the branch with their help. I was fortunate that I was not charged for their callout. A lesson learnt, and another very protective spiritual Father in whom I am grateful.

The 20,000 volts could have killed me, but He had other ideas. The homeowner was also very gracious in helping me, and not only that, I had underestimated the time it took and the number of truckloads needed to remove the spoil; which amounted to 4 truckloads of 3 cubic meters. It was a very big job, and she agreed to pay an extra $200 to cover my costs. She was not obliged to do so but was happy to see the trees gone.

Life can be unkind at times, as incidents like this always appear to bring your life or your career to an end, as you may have grasped by now, but some have their funny side. I had two customers about half-way up their steep streets at Belair; and I had a truck which had a tail-shaft emergency brake which was almost useless and needed to be adjusted weekly. This first example was laughable as I was wearing canvas Army boots, and with the truck parked near the bottom of the street on a rainy day, I walked/climbed to near the top of the street for my customers pickup, and on leaving the house, the street was so slippery, I hung onto my two wheeled trolley with the heavy bag on it and skied/slid down the hill to the truck. I laughed all the way down, about 30 meters. The other, the customer was halfway up a hill, and I would drive up the hill and stop alongside his driveway, and do what any good driver would do and turn the front wheels into the kerb to assist the hand brake hold the vehicle. To explain how I did the job, I needed to turn the engine off and on with an ignition key on the left side and rear of the cab near the hoist. I left the truck out of gear so I could operate the hydraulic hoist on the side of the truck and lower it to the ground. I then went onto the property to change the bag over and take the full bag to the truck. Fortunately, at this house the bag was in the driveway at the front of the house. While I was changing the bag, I could hear the brake slipping, and so I hurried to get to the truck. Then I saw that the front tyre was starting to creep over the kerb. I operated the hoist and threw the bag over the top into the truck as the tyre lifted onto the footpath. Whenever I park the truck, I never shut the driver's door to save the latch, so getting into the cab is easier, but here is the hard bit, the door closed on me with me standing on the running board. I very rarely swear, but this time I did as the truck on full lock took off across the road on this steep hill with me riding it. All I could see was the truck tipping over and emptying the load down the hill and destroying the vehicle. I was so relieved when it stopped against the opposite kerb, that I got into the truck totally embarrassed, and drove madly up the hill, my body shaking. There was a miracle here, firstly, God is in charge, secondly, I had replaced a very loose tipper hinge at the rear of the truck bin on the right-hand side exactly one week before. Had that not happened and the loose hinge not been replaced the truck would definitely have tipped over from a broken hinge. Life then continued on as normal. God is Great, regardless of the circumstances, He saves.....

16

Another Life Changing Event

I am here looking at this Imac screen pondering how to introduce this chapter, the contents of which are a severe embarrassment to me, but an event which occurred changed my life forever, but not in the same way as the Life Changer in Chapter 4. This was the opposite. As a Christian and an ex-police member the implications could be indeed frightening.

You have read of my mistakes and difficulties and may now have been made aware of my failings and emotional struggles, if not an almost inability to keep my mind on track. I am certainly aware of these. I believe now that, psychologically, I was a mess.

The events of one particular day, in 1993, I now relate. I was visiting my usual customers, and I was tempted to act inappropriately with a particular customer, but emotionally I felt that this should not happen, so I desisted. At the same time, something happened, which could have been conviction, but a dizziness came upon me which made me realise that my actions in being tempted, caused an emotional fog over me. I couldn't get away quick enough. Perhaps this was the Father offering me a way out. I left there, realising that my gas tank in the truck was almost empty, (I ran the truck on natural gas), and so I needed to refill the tank at the next service station. If

I did not, the truck could be difficult to start as the gas pressure was low. I then attended a service station nearby and drove the truck alongside the row of pumps containing the gas pump, but could not get to it as a car was parked at the front petrol pump. I waited a full 10 minutes for the driver to return to his car, assuming he was only paying for his fuel, but he did not return. I even went into the Servo shop, but he was not there, so I asked the attendant being quite angry and frustrated, "Where is the driver of the car in front of my truck."

He said, "I've no idea mate, you'll just have to wait." I stormed back to the truck, with my patience at boiling point, climbed into the cab, and stewed. I was emotionally erratic, quite agitated, and angry over this matter, so it must have been guilt hitting me hard. Eventually, after about 10 minutes the driver returned with two young children. As he was putting a young child in his car, I leaned out of my window, and said, "Thanks for your consideration, where have you been?" He responded by yelling back at me in an abusive fashion, throwing responsibility back on me. He was shaking his fist angrily. It is interesting to note I can never recall what he said, to do so, in my mind I had the fear of repeating what I did next.

Breakdown

I just exploded in rage, there being no excuse here at all, suddenly, with no thought of repercussions, my inability to handle confrontation took over, and I used the power of the truck to ram his car away from the pumps. I then got out of the truck and my rage had me chase him around the tarmac and I laid into him assaulting him. I had lost control. I am loath to include one detail which must be said, which made the event so serious, that by God's grace, the possible result did not happen, thankfully. The car driver was carrying his 18-month-old daughter as his young son was getting in the car. My rage was such it was impossible for me to see any outcome or make a better decision. Although disputed in court, he dropped his daughter to the ground and as a result of me driving forward the girl ended up under my truck having missed running over her with the front wheel of the truck by a very small margin. I still have emotional difficulties of this result in my heart. That burden was hard to carry for years afterwards. You may be asking the question; "You have testified of your faith in God, how could this have happened?" I agree, that is why I have included much of my weaknesses in falling away.

It wasn't long before a police patrol arrived, and I was arrested and taken to the city police watch house for questioning. Suddenly I realised that I was broken and totally empty inside my Spirit, having to accept what my future may hold. I was signed in at the Watch house, fingerprinted, and held in an interview room for questioning. This situation was now in total opposition to what my career of 22 years before me said as I had done this many, many, times in that era. My mental state now was a total blank as to what happened at this time, and this created a depression where I was non-compos (lost composure) and could not think. I died inside, accepting my fate where I knew where I was going and what would occur, only mechanically. I was charged with, 1. Act endanger life, 2. Assault, and 3. Property damage. I was then bailed to appear the following day in the Adelaide Magistrates Court.

I was able to contact my pastor, Reg, at our church, who obliged me by attending at the police cells and transporting me back to my truck after I was bailed, and also to encourage me as I was still in shock. I was then able to drive the truck home. Reg had, I believe now, also contacted Pauline and told her he would assist us. With some grace, on my arrest, the police allowed me to refuel the truck but to leave it there until it could be removed from the property.

In retrospect, two decisions which could have made a difference to any court penalty was the official caution prior to any questioning which was given. I was still in shock at this time, and answered no questions, it was just too hard. I believe that this was a mistake, as had I told the exact story, any assessment of my personality or truthfulness by the court, could have been different. The other was once again an inability to assess any results, was to obtain the service station video which could have been available to be put before the Court. As an ex-policeman, I should have known this, as it would have changed and supported my evidence, although also proved my guilt towards a more severe sentence. I found out later that the car driver in the incident was an off-duty Policeman, which means that the offences I committed would be treated more severely.

Once I had been placed before the magistrate's court for the official charges to be laid, a day or so later, I was able to have a Solicitor represent me. A young man of little experience in trials by jury, who actually offered me a Barrister, which I declined, another mistake. I pleaded not guilty and was arraigned for trial by jury in June 1994, which will be explained later in this chapter. Had I been advised correctly, I would have pleaded guilty, but I wanted my story to be told.

Pastor Dean who was the pastor in charge at the time in my church, was incredibly supportive, and he told the congregation of my dilemma. The love I felt from other members was very encouraging over what I had done, minus detail to them, with no condemnation at all. I did receive counselling and support from Dean and Reg, this also applied to my family who supported me and loved on me totally. The incident of course was a huge shock to them, they took it well, as they were of mature age at the time and our relationship was very good.

I have no idea now, as to why I wanted to improve the business after this event. I had been using my truck, the old Dodge 3 tonner, for 9 years, the cab was rusting, and the hoist was wearing out, so I decided to buy a Compactor 12 tonne truck. After test driving an International cab over, I decided it was too big and really could not afford to run it.

So, in May, realising the court case was in late June, I checked the truck advertising pages on the internet and found a used Leyland Compactor for a reasonable price, but in New South Wales. My son Adrian was quite happy to travel with me to Coonabarabran, to examine the vehicle, and we travelled by bus to get there. The vehicle was a cab over, 6-cylinder English Leyland, with an Alison Auto transmission, single axle drive. The vehicle drove OK, but was a slow goer, but as we had travelled so far, and that it did have an NSW certificate of roadworthiness, I decided to buy it. Adrian gained a learner's licence to drive it on learner plates to help me get it home. We headed off late in the evening to return to Adelaide via Broken

Hill, hoping it would get us there. It is a long trip, and Adrian was driving when a kangaroo jumped the road head on into our lights. Adrian hit the brakes in an attempt to avoid the animal, (which a driver should never do, especially in a truck.) we hit it, of course, and stopped to check for damage. It was a large roo and had damaged the right front corner of the truck. What actually happened was that we went to drive off and couldn't, in applying the brakes heavily, the brakes air system malfunctioned and jammed the rear brakes on which is a safety feature. Had I realised a simple fix was to un-adjust the rear brakes to free them we could have driven on, but without brakes. Not a good idea, but I did not have the means anyway.

This happened at 1.00am, and my attempts at waving down a semi-trailer for assistance was proving fruitless. After 2 or 3 went past, one did stop. The drivers radio communication among themselves must have indicated that we were in trouble. The driver may not have been in a position to fix the brakes, so he gave me a ride into Broken Hill, while Adrian stayed with the truck.

This is where I was glad to be a member of the RAA road Service in Adelaide, even though I needed to wait until after daylight at the RAA service centre and workshop - my emergency did not encourage an early opening for my assistance - even with Adrian waiting in the truck 100km back on the road. When it did happen, the mechanic and I drove back to the truck where he repaired the brake slave cylinder so we could carry on our trip. The RAA were good enough to honour our dilemma and they even paid the service fee of $300.

The other idea which I took on was to lease 200 customers from another person to assist him. This I did, which boosted our income, without any thought of what penalty I may receive in my court case. I assumed that I would get a suspended sentence, which kept my mind on track to continue running the business for the ensuing 6 months to my court date. I must have been trying to put the whole event behind me and carry on as normal not considering that I may not be able to run the business at all should I receive a prison sentence. It did not occur to me. Yes, it's what is called denial.... I mention this story to indicate a mindset hiding my emotional state towards a false normality at the same time taking on a faith in God in hope of a positive result, out of my normal positivity. With the support of my family and the Church, I continued to operate the business, at the same time preparing the compactor to operate with my hoist attached but modified to fit on the rear compaction door/bin. The old Dodge still needed to be used until the compactor was finished.

The Court Case

Having been through the process of the Magistrates court, and pleading 'not guilty' the supreme court trial days arrived. There were a few adjournments, prior to actual trial by jury, so on the actual day on 22/6/94, the plea of 'not guilty' plea applied to the main charge, but the other two I pleaded 'guilty'.

Pauline was with me, and we, being early, walked around the market for a while, and still feeling confident, a bought a used citizen electronic watch, from a money lender/used jewellery vendor. I mention this as it kept my mind off my upcoming trial. I still have the watch, and after only putting 2 or 3 batteries in it since 1994, it only stopped working in 2019. A quick conversation with my Solicitor, and after a short time my name was called, and we entered the courtroom with Pauline following. Thankfully, in writing this report, the details of the case are vague, apart from the aggrieved party, and one or two witnesses who were called to give evidence. The one thing I do recall was that the plaintiff's story was different to mine, but he, being a police constable, was believed rather than my testimony. Eventually, I was called to give my story, where the fine details which I mentioned obviously were not believed. Two points which were not mentioned regarding my character was my police service and Christian faith, which should have been. When my Solicitor was giving his defence arguments after all witnesses had been called, I expected him to put forward a certain aspect of my character, (I am unsure now what that was,) my jaw dropped but I was unable to get his attention.

The Judge, who I add at this time was a senior female, addressed the jury as to the case, and they then retired for their verdict. I was placed in a holding cell, while the Jury were deliberating, until 4pm, after 3 and a half hours they returned with a unanimous verdict of 'guilty'. The trial was then adjourned to 29/6/94 for sentencing. Bail continuing.

The Shock and the Trauma

The day arrived. With Pauline, and perhaps a few friends at the court, a day which could change our family for life, I was feeling quite afraid but confident of a positive result. This did not happen as in reality I resolved my fate should I receive a custodial sentence. I needed to be prepared but I wasn't. I took my place in the dock, as the Judge read the penalties. "On the first count of 'Endangering life', 2 years Imprisonment....", for the charge of 'Damaging property' 9 months imprisonment, and for 'Assault' 4 months, with a non-parole period of 10 months. On hearing that I just yelled out, "No, please suspend it...". The shock wave went through me like a lightning bolt, and I fainted in the dock. The two court orderlies caught me and assisted me from the dock and escorted me from the courtroom and placed me in a holding cell. In doing so, I collapsed on the floor totally devastated with tears pouring from my face, I was terrified. All I could do was to cry out to my Lord Jesus.... "Lord, I have nothing, I am all yours now..."

Many people reading this may relate, but this is a point where the world around me died, I was emptied spiritually, I died inside, totally numb, suddenly my life was ripped apart, where else could I go emotionally but to the only power I knew, that Jesus with whom I joined those 20 years ago. Thought evaded me as I waited for what was going to happen. My time came as the guards picked me up from the floor and guided me from the holding area and placed me in a large prison van which was divided into two sections of steel cage. There were two other inmates in the front section, with me in the back section, alone. They did not acknowledge me nor speak to me as they were chatting and laughing together. In a short time, the van moved off and all I could do was sit and feel apprehensive.

I did not even think or contemplate where we were going, I realised that I was in the hands of someone else and must accept my fate, as I had no idea, not having been to the Northfield jail complex before, except 30 years earlier in police training. The van, on arrival, drove through the main jail gate, and we 3 were escorted from the van to the administration office through the very old, large wooden doors. The other two were sent through quickly, and when my name was called I was ushered into the manager's office to sit down. The senior uniformed man ran through the details of my charges and instructed me on procedures. I remained mute under my apprehensive mood, and he asked me if I had anything to say. I responded by saying, "I believe you should know that I was a police constable until I resigned in 1985." He responded, "Do you need protection?" I replied, "No." I knew that my protection was in Jesus and His Holy Spirit, so that was my confidence. Once the admin details were settled, I was escorted between two guards across a courtyard in front of the main building 'B' division, to the high security 'E' division. At this point, I had the distinct impression of the warmth of the Holy Spirit presence, as we walked, and I felt totally confident albeit empty of emotion.

17

Prison Life

I was taken into the 'E' division through a small exercise yard with 2 sections of barred cell blocks of 10 cells. Each cell housed 2 inmates each. The door to the first cell block was opened by the guard, and I was ushered inside and then the door to the first cell on the left was opened and I was introduced to my cell mate. My heart jumped as I was confronted by a tall, lanky man of about 40 years, tattooed, bearded, and with long hair. His appearance inspired me to believe I was looking at a tough, fierce, criminal type that should be feared. So, when he spoke, I immediately relaxed as he held out his hand with a smile and introduced himself. The door slammed behind us, and I stood transfixed as he explained procedure in the wing, and said, "So, you are a new boy, I'll look after to you, stick with me." This I did, like glue.

At this point, I can either guess some of the procedure, or tizzy it up for the sake of readability, or accept that my memory has faded. The detail is unnecessary anyway. I will say that the meals were very good, one of which came along fairly quickly, as all of the area was opened up during the afternoon, where I was escorted among the crowd of men, whose offences were serious, some being lifers. I found here a respect from the others as I respected them, but conversation was scarce, as they would have been aware that I was only here for assessment by the guards, as a newbie. They just ignored me really, perhaps eyeing me up and down.

What surprised me was that my cellmate trusted me implicitly, as he shared lockdown communication between the cells, and the reasons for it. I soon realised that the prison grapevine must have been very good, as you may recall I offended against an off-duty policeman. Maybe this could be why I was respected and trusted. I made sure that I kept my mouth shut and took a back seat in the system to maintain that trust. I now understand why prison sentences and removal from society are considered punishment. Life in this division could be soul destroying, as freedom does not exist, and appeared to me to lack any form of objectivity. Life here was very regulated, with daily exercise in this interior space. Once again, my memory is short as to whether we saw sunshine in this wing for exercise, although a must for health. We had no private clothing, and all cleaning was done in the prison by trustees. All meals were cooked in the prison kitchen, also by trusties.

After 2 weeks in 'E' division, not experiencing any incidents whatsoever, my time there was purely for assessment, and my cell mate certainly cared for me. I was at peace, but a strange peace considering where I was. I was transferred to 'B' division on the third floor of the main building, so I must have behaved well enough to have a good report. 'B' division was a much larger area. It catered for more prisoners, and my floor was considered as part of the workshop construction area, where daily trips to workshops occurred, and work performed for the public service areas, such as housing trust, as a money earner for the Government.

This cell area only catered for one person per cell, to my relief, and I was amazed when I was led to my cell in this area, to read my prison number above the door. I wept, as the number read 88840. In referring to Chapter 6 on Bible Numerics, the number 8 is new beginnings, and by putting 3 together the Hebrew Language has it read as Jesus name. The number 40 being testing. So that immediately lifted my confidence to a higher level as I knew the Holy Spirit resided in that cell with me. The guard instructed me as to the rules of the section, including meal and lock down times, also an allowance of cash per day, access to outside telephone calls on a schedule, and for applications to have goods imported into the prison for use in the cell. My desire was to have my bible imported for study purposes. The difference here compared with 'E' division was that we had a large outside exercise yard. Over the next few days, I was able to get to know the other inmates, and once again it was obvious that they knew who I offended against, as I received the same trust and respect. It was also obvious that they did not know I was an ex-policeman otherwise I may have been treated differently. There was a prisoner in this section who was a lifer, and his cell was loaded with books and a computer. He said he was studying to be a priest, and my impression of him and his attitude was that he was not of that ilk, and also that the other prisoners all gave him a hard time, not having any respect for him. For me, it did not take long to show them, by my actions and attitude, my faith, hence their respect for me. Once I received my bible, the Lord inspired to me Psalm 37, and with paper and pen, I wrote the positive verses of that psalm over and over. A few of the prisoners were very interested in what I was doing in the times that we were in unlock mode and wanted to read the verses I had written. This was the start of a mini prayer/discussion group within the cell block, as these men indicated that they had fallen from grace in their faith, so I was able to encourage them. Just one reason why I was there.

Another reason, which can be expected, is relationships. On one free day I was alone in the cell block with another inmate who was one of the few men who were gym regulars. He was a tall and strong man. In conversation, he said that he was serving a sentence for armed robbery. He came to me and asked me to do a favour for him, as he had some back pain. He explained that he wanted me to do a 'drop' for him to correct a slipped disc in his spine. I had no idea what he was talking about, so he explained that he would cross his arms across his chest, and I was to come behind him and hold him in my arms under his arms, lift him, and without his feet touching the floor, 'drop' him in a jerking motion. I did this and I heard a crack which did exactly what he was hoping for. Acceptance in prison is not often rewarded, relationships depend on similar interests and attainments. James I will call him, immediately befriended me, and rewarded me by drawing me into a closer relationship with other inmates. Conversation increased where much was shared including trust regarding the underside of prison life. The biggest attainment for me was that I was introduced to the gymnasium, where James trained me in the operation of the machines including the boxing ball and it's timing. I had already used one or two machines in the gym beforehand and I was basically ignored personally until this incident.

Another conversation with one of the gym 'team' made me realise even more the trust that they had in me. At regular intervals the guards would go through the cell blocks while we were in the workshops, and strip search our cells by pulling beds and personal items, if we had any, apart in the search for contraband and drug items. I was always found to be 'clean' but asked appropriate questions for them. I was always silent. This young man was housed opposite me, and many times, as I was doing my bible reading in my cell, I noticed that his light was on. Now this guy was a short human 'A' frame who frequented the gym consistently. When we had a conversation sometime later, I mentioned to him this fact, so I asked him why.

"That's when I do me drugs", he said.

"That's when I am reading my Bible".

"Yeah, I know." Our conversation continued, even into my sharing my faith with him. I realised then that here was another reason why I was there. I even asked him how it was possible to hide the drugs considering the cell searches. He responded by showing me, it was obvious the trust he had in me.

Workshop and Security Demeanours

The workshop was open to inmates with skills, my skills were in carpentry, welding, and building, including concreting. The only skills I could use here was timber and welding. I still volunteered, and to be honest, I have no idea now what I did there apart from general assistance as a tool man. My reason for mentioning this part of Prison life was to indicate what was done in the workshops and the demeaning security checks on returning to the cells at the end of the day.

The main work that I can recollect being done there was the construction of gun safes from 25mm steel plate built by men with those skills in welding and the use of the steel bending machines. I was enthralled in watching how this steel was cut, bent, and welded with the massive machinery needed. The lighter work done was in the construction of galvanised tin waste bins used in schools and housing trust houses, and even sold in hardware stores. They were all cut from flat steel sheets and shaped and rolled in machinery designed for the purpose. I was in awe of the man given the task of rolling and shaping the lids into a slight cone. A sheet of tin placed in a lathe and a tool shaped alike a baseball bat used to force the tin into that curved shape and then edged. The only job I can recall was rolling the edges of the bins.

The food, I was amazed that all of us were not obese, with the massive amount of food supplied. Far better than at home, but the quantity indicated that the cost of housing and keeping prisoners under lock and key was very high. Three meals a day, 6 am, midday, and 4pm. In the workshops, morning tea was pies and pasties, masses of them. Definitely encouragement not to complain but be satisfied in having your stomach filled.

I now mention visiting day, because of the demeaning security measures when leaving insecure areas to go to the secure areas. My very first visit from outside apart from family, was from a woman from my Christian church at that time whom I had never met. She and her family were new to the church. Pastor Dean, after my internment, addressed the body supporting me, as we were very good friends, apparently my case had stirred the congregation into interceding for me in my dilemma, hence this visit. The system was that only certain days during the week were allocated for visits from family and friends for the inmates. As the prison population was high, face to face visits were well guarded so some personal contact was closely watched. Security was also high, so when my visit time came to an end, 15 minutes to half an hour, I was escorted back though the barrier.

I only mention this section of the story, to indicate what I went through for the sake of showing a degree of humiliation. In both areas I was required to strip and have my underclothes searched, so no tools could be removed from the workshops, or drug paraphernalia smuggled into the jail from the visitors, which was the main concern. The guard who searched me when leaving the visiting area was the only guard to give me a hard time. He always had a comment to make to demean me further. I ignored him. It was rumoured that he was an ex-CIB Detective, so I assumed he knew of me, but thankfully never mentioned my police history. Had he done so my story could have been very different.

Life in the prison continued as the acceptance of my internment and the presence of God in my life made my life there quite tolerable. It certainly appeared that I was being used of God to be a witness for Him in loving and accepting of all in the jail and coming alongside of them. They knew I was dedicated to my faith and accepted me in that circle. This next section will show God's hand in my early release.

The Parole Board

After 8 weeks of behavioural assessment, which is the norm, I was called up to attend a parole board meeting, where they had adjudicated my ability to be rehabilitated, as the results of my behaviour and acceptance of my internment. This happened early September 94, and I was escorted to the administration area to attend the meeting. I was very apprehensive, not knowing procedures, or anything about the 'Board'. I was shown into a large room, and my eyes looked into the gloom at a large table with people seated around it, with one person at the head. Scary actually. Then I heard a voice, "Hi Graham. My eyes focused onto the voice in recognition, and I immediately felt embarrassed, as I said, "Hi, Gus?" My chin dropped and eyes widened as I recognised him.

I am loath to explain this, as not wanting to put him in a bad place by his obvious relationship with the legal system in the prison, but it is now 26 years later and that board would now be consisting of different people, and Gus would now be well retired, so he would not be placed under scrutiny at all. At the same time, he would hopefully have explained his relationship with me to the Board beforehand. We were close friends in our younger years, drinking mates if you like, and both involved in the C.M.F. Army at the same time. He also married a woman known to both of us, and she was a part time soldier as well. There was conversation in the board room, of which I never heard really. Once the meeting was over, I was escorted back to 'B' division where I was told by the guard to pack my bags and wait in a collection area. It was decided that I would be transferred to the prison farm at Berri in the Riverland. I was very happy about that which was the first step to release, but it meant total separation from family and friends. I was ready and waiting in the release area along with another young inmate who obviously would be travelling with me. This young man was the only person who actually did not take to my faith and was not receptive. While waiting, I was very surprised when Gus approached me privately. He had spoken about me to the other board members, and a decision was made to change the decision as to where I was to go.

Divine Intervention

Gus then told me, "As you are running a business, and going to Berri would create too much hardship with that, also that your aptitude has been assessed as trustworthy, I have arranged to have you moved to the release cottages, for weekend release to help Pauline run the business." My reaction was in amazement as emotionally I was so relieved that I almost collapsed. I could not thank him enough for his intervention. Tears flowed. This was a Divine arrangement where the Lord had Gus on that board to assist me for my future. It was pure miracle; no man could arrange that. Gus left after a short 'good to see you' handshake. I walked back to where that young man was waiting. I burst into tears again as I told him, "Don't you ever tell me there is no God..... I am going home." The look on his face showed shock and amazement, as I was wheeled away by the guard who took hold of me and escorted to a vehicle where we drove to the pre-release cottages east of the main prison and shown to my new 'quarters'. In writing this, I needed to check 'Google Earth' as to more detail to refresh my memory. The years have shown many changes since I was there, six Cottages housed four detainees each, two of them housed Paedophiles. Rations were distributed according to personal orders, as each person was responsible for feeding themselves, once a week from the admin offices. The area consisted of a market garden with glass houses and vegetable beds, a poultry area for chickens and egg production. This garden and environ was used to supply a large quantity of produce to the prison, as well as this pre-release centre. The 'Peds' were responsible for the market garden and with assistance by the other two cottages which included me. An Aboriginal man was responsible for the Chicken 'farm'. I was housed with two other inmates, and it was arranged between us who would cook meals. house cleaning was also our responsibility. I was unaware how long I was to be here, possibly until my non-parole period expired, which would be 9 months from my date of internment, the end of March 1995. Paul and Andy, my room mates were easy to get on with although Andy was out working during the day, and Paul and I were doing odd jobs in the area. After a time, when we trusted each other, we shared our internment reasons. He was in for arson, so I sympathised as he did not light the match as told.

A Light at the End of the Tunnel

My first weekend approached, while old friend Ian would collect me on the Saturday morning and take me home to work on my business, but only in administration to assist in the management of the bag men working for us on my behalf. It did not take long for the work to get out among our friends and the Church, where God was given the glory for getting me to this stage. It was a great deep breath of fresh air to be home with the family. I could not drive nor leave the property but being home was very OK. Come Sunday night, Ian would return me to the cottages for the next week, where life was regulated. Contact with the other cottage inmates was intermittent depending on the jobs. The Peds were left alone. The food supply was abundant, similar to 'B' division, but on order, so food was never an issue. Life here was very comfortable. Paul and I got on very well and became good friends and have actually we met a couple of times, once our terms were served. I must assume here that the administrators must have considered me a trustee, as I was given a job outside of the prison perimeter. A fencing contractor was given the job of installing a sheep fence around the eastern and northern boundaries of the prison area. I was chosen to work with him for two weeks solid. I would make myself lunch from the cottage supplies and was collected by him in his Land Rover in the morning and dropped off at night. The Contractor, Evan, taught me how to build these fences which assisted me many years later when I worked on a friend's 45-acre property for 18 months building a considerable number of the same fences. It was a great learning experience for a future purpose.

One aspect of rehabilitation in prison is meant to be psychological counselling. Only once did this occur, and that was while in the cottages. A young man and I had a conversation about my internment and about my conditioning where I may have blurted out some of my hurt etc, but really offered me very little advice, except that he gave me a book to go through which would help in organising my life. That night I skipped through this book, which included pictures and guidance on discipline. I immediately noticed that it painted a picture of New Age spirituality, and the exercises needed were so disciplined, that in no way could any person living a lifestyle where incarceration was needed may want to or even try to achieve it. It certainly did not fit my social skills. This is my personal opinion only. But the one thing I did get out of it was I taught myself to totally relax, not through the relaxation mentioned in the book, but purely in lying on my bed and 'relaxing'. I had the peace of our Lord Jesus of course. Time went slowly here.

18

On the Way Home

I spent only six weeks in the cottages area, after eight weeks in 'B' division, a total of 14 weeks internment, which took me to mid-October. Surprise was in store, as being the good boy that I was, administration decided, considering my non-parole period of nine months, that I was to be released on home detention. The actual date of the non-parole period being the end of March 1995. I still shake my head in not understanding the wonder of the authority of our Lord as to do what He wants, for this miraculous change in events, for my release. There was a catch, however, this was a very strict regime, where if I failed, I could be sent back to 'B' division to start again. The administration were giving me a chance in testing me as to my reliability. I was to carry with me a beeper, so when I was called, I must answer the phone in my home to respond to that call and speak to my Parole Officer. This created a small problem. Our property was of one acre, and it took more than 5 minutes to respond to that call if I was in my workshop.

I was caught three times, and it took a visit from the Parole Officer to straighten me out. I had to buy a hands-free phone to carry with me. Just one mistake had me test the system by not fully understanding the system. One time I went for a walk off our property within the 200-metre range of the beeper, which was too far from the phone. Boy did I get told that if I missed again, I would be going back. Thankfully, this did not happen. So, there I was, able to catch up with work on our block and support Pauline in the operation of the business. So once again life went on, and in January 1995, I was released on a good behaviour bond until the end of my sentence in June 1996.

This time of my life was the hardest to accept, a downfall of epic proportions. How and why did I do this, which resulted in a penalty which took away my freedom. This era is one reason why I am writing this biography, as a testimony of God's grace in my life where any person can place their life in His hands and be freed from their difficulties or drawn through them. One factor which always hounded me at this time, which could mean too much pride which needed to be knocked out of me, was that as a born-again believer and an ex-police member, should need to be humbled as I was. Jesus grabbed me by the scruff of my neck and said, "*Graham, come back here I want you to stay with me...*"

Psalm 94;12, "Blessed is the man who You do chasten, O Lord, and do teach from Your Law". Don't go away, this is not the end. I still have a lot to learn.

Another Era Starts

It started in 1997, when I sold the rubbish removal business mentioned in Chapter 14, and was employed in private enterprise, a locally run bus company. The reason for the sale, was due to the old English diesel engine failing for a second time, as a lack of knowledge of the mechanical requirements regarding the type of coolant required to prevent the wet sleeve corrosion. It cost me $4000 to recondition the engine the first time, so when the engine blew the second time after two years, that was the end of it. It was at the end of a day's work and I was driving the truck, lumbering up South Road O'Halloran Hill, when suddenly the engine slowed, and I noticed a cloud of steam and boiling water streaming out of the radiator water storage bottle behind the cab. I screamed in delight, yelling, "Thank you Lord, I'm out of here...." A strange thing to say when your engine fails, but I was so tired, and actually relieved that I could get away from the hard work of operating the business. Tired, which affected my psyche towards frustration and short temper, harming, in a small way, my family relationships. I will add that I loved the family dearly, but I was a grumpy sod still susceptible to angry outbursts.

Having somehow managed to get the truck home, I parked it at the bottom of the block and then went to tell Pauline the sad but good news. I then had the problem of getting rid of a compactor full of rubbish. The next day I started the engine which necessitated the emptying of that load onto the block and hiring a truck and back-hoe tractor to cart it away. A costly removal.

We were friendly with a couple, Jim and his wife, at our local Church at that time, and he was a diesel mechanic working at a local bus company, so he assisted me in repairing the engine at home getting it running again. In the meantime, I leased my customers to other operators which kept some money coming in, while we worked together on the engine.

As I had a licence to drive passenger buses, he suggested that I apply to the bus company for a job. I did just that and I was given the job of working with Jim for a year in the company workshop, servicing the fleet of twelve large, fifty seat vehicles, before I actually was offered the job of bus driver.

It did not take me long in the job to realise that the owner of the company needed to be approached as if treading on eggshells. Among the family of drivers there was an air of disrespect for him. For me, being a shy quiet individual (?), I kept my office visits to a bare minimum. I needed to be very careful considering my history. Apart from the above statement, I did enjoy this job, but failed in a few areas where I received the brunt of the director's anger, mainly through his misunderstanding of the events and what actually happened, bar one.

Oh No, Not Again!

This book is written with the object of a testimony of God's grace in my life, and not a list of discrepancies I may have been involved in. But the good graces which erupt from the ashes of the events in the story; a comparison made between a life of not knowing the Love of God, as I was prior to 1975, until a life of confessing that life as bad news to God and accepting his grace. I always reflect on what my life would have been now, had I not made that decision. I would be dead by now. This statement is not made to justify mistakes and repercussions made under grace, but that of weakness in not understanding that grace and its rewards.

The pressure of the responsibility of driving buses and carrying passengers adds up over a long period; the following two years saw me being treated very well by the director in him giving me every opportunity to prove myself as a responsible driver, in several areas of the company so he could direct me into the best area of my expertise. These included:

1. Six months on an airport to city hotel's permanent run.

2. A three bus military convoy passenger run to Port Augusta and return empty.

3. A university geology hire to Murray Bridge. I did what any driver would do when feeling sleepy on the return trip, by stopping on the roadside to rest by walking around the bus. A legitimate safety concern. I was not used again for this type of hire.

4. An Interstate run to Melbourne, which was overnight. Rest stops were required, but on arrival in Melbourne I could not read a roadmap due to an eyesight difficulty. The constant night drive had my vision set on the road within the area of the headlights, and close vision would not reset to reading mode. So, I actually needed to stop the bus on the freeway, and ask the director of the group, who was the night manager for the Hilton Hotel, to read the map and direct me to the house where we were to stay for the weekend. This contract was for a Filipino group to play an interstate match of 10 pin bowling against a Melbourne team. It was a weekend stopover; and once settled I was looked after well by my hosts with a good rest. I can understand the reason why I was not given a second chance on this job, as on leaving Melbourne, I took the wrong lane not being aware of the highway split and ended up in Geelong. I was not used again on interstate runs.

5. A year or more used for school runs, where student noise in the

buses caused stresses, which caused me to stop the bus and address either the students or the adult in charge.

6. I was the first driver to be used on a new contract of a dedicated public run. I lasted one year when I realised, I was losing concentration and requested that I be removed from the run, as I was becoming careless.

7. The final straw in my bus driving career occurred while employed on minor school contracts on a particular night while driving a mid-sized Mercedes bus.

You may understand from this listing, that I was not necessarily a driver capable of handling long hours behind the wheel and so I may have deserved the director's criticisms. But on this particular night, while transporting the school students, I turned the vehicle radio off due to the constant loud noise of the conversations and could not hear it anyway. Once I had offloaded the students at their school, I drove back to the depot, forgetting to turn the radio on again. I was also very tired at this time as it was a long day. On arrival at the depot, it was my duty to clean the bus and refuel it. It was about 10.00pm at the time. I had just finished refuelling the bus when the director came almost running towards me yelling loudly and waving his torch around, accusing me of not responding to his radio calls.

This situation was very similar to the incident which caused my demise quoted in Chapter 16 in 1993. I was stunned, and I reacted in such a way that I seemed to lack control and I assaulted him by lashing out at him. To my utter bewilderment, I have never really understood how it happened, but assume it was a spiritual movement. I did not tense, I felt nothing, I actually did not make a deliberate decision to assault him, a pure reaction to abuse.

Another Penalty

I hesitate here to mention any detail of this event, as I am deeply ashamed and in regret at my behaviour as I recall it. It serves no purpose to relate the finale except that the next day I phoned the local police station and was told that the director had reported the event as he had sustained injury. I then attended at the bus depot and apologised to him for my actions. I was immediately sacked.

As a result of his complaint, on 25/10/2000, I was charged with "assault occasioning bodily harm" and convicted, with a sentence of 10 months imprisonment, suspended on entering into a bond for two years which included attending an anger management course, and 120 hours of community service. I was very fortunate on this occasion that the director did not sue me for damages which could have been a very real possibility.

I did sign up for the anger management course, and the community service, run by the prison service, which proved to be quite valuable, and I did the same within the Christian community, where the strength of prayer ministry did a mighty job in including the power of God's Holy Spirit which brought about a release. It was Theophostic in nature which broke down the areas of the emotions being affected by PTSD, which put up a soul tie barrier in the memory of the incident. It was akin to psychiatric but with deep spiritual prayer association. This proved to be very successful where I was released from the guilt of the events, and a barrier in my mind which hid the emotional coping side of the guilt.

A light-hearted note here, where the person in charge of the community service section of the prison system, which involved working with other parolees in public clean-up programs, was a man well known to me who, not only was a war veteran, but an old customer of mine in my business. God has a sense of humour. This also made me aware of the condition of PTSD, which John had, and I made an effort to assist him spiritually. We got on well even though he always threw away my attempts, laughing and joking in ridicule. I just let that bounce off me. There is always a reason why God puts us in situations, not just for our benefit but for the people we deal with. One particular incident with him, where having lost my driver's licence in 1994, I asked John to drive me to an appointment. He waited in the car during the appointment. When I got into the car after the appointment, he was asleep, so I got into the car, even slamming the door, this did not wake him; so being surprised at this, I rocked the car sideways to get a reaction. I got one. Suddenly he woke up, sat bolt upright arms up in a defensive pose eyes wide open, head turning from side to side taking deep breaths.

He was in shock and then he said, "Don't do that, what happened ******(expletives)****".

"Sorry mate, I just got in the car, I was trying to wake you...." I understood then, the impact of PTSD on a man's spirit as a returned soldier. Recently, in speaking with my Doctor, in relating my concerns regarding my occasional health conditions, that he suggested I may still have signs of PTSD as a result of the 1993 and 2001 episodes. I have never actually followed up on that.

What can I say here? That in mentioning these dramas in my life, that has any bearing in His glory in developing a better attitude in me. Firstly, my attention was drawn to me needing the help offered by the conviction psychologically within the system, which certainly had me assessing my own public attitudes and in developing a closer walk with God. This is always what He wants from His church.

The year 2000 brought about two events, the tragic repeat of a breakdown in control over violence and its penalties, once again gaining the support of the Christian church people in encouraging myself and family to stability.

Secondly, I was placed in a situation where I was working with other parolees and with my supervisor John, whom I was able to support in his efforts to supervise them. I was also able to develop relationships as a witness for the peace that I was given by Him even under these conditions. Although, having been a member of the police department, I was fully aware of the problems people have in criminal activity, to actually work with and live with offenders was an eye opener as to their hopelessness. For me, the whole situation was very humbling, and I was able to enjoy the experience. This went on for a number of months until I was released back into the community.

Now, there was a process of settling back into 'normal' life with the family, in raising our three children, and maintaining our home. A life of sitting back and just looking at other options. It was necessary to apply to Centrelink for job seeker allowance. A long way to go for a retirement pension, so looking for work was the only option.

19

Employment in Retirement

Now an entry into a totally different lifestyle of employment. I will take you on a tour of my new work life which proved to be very different from my past work life. Firstly, a visit to Centrelink to apply for unemployment benefits, which included searching for work, attending classes to aid job applications, and then searching. At this time, I was 60 years of age, and not entitled for the age pension just yet, so the search was on, but only for about two years.

The jobs included selling office supplies, which lasted only a few days, driving blue plate taxis which lasted eight months, a trip to a cattle station off the Strzelecki track via Lyndhurst as a welder, a disaster lasting two days, and then an entry into the building trade which lasted eight years, interspersed with professional passenger carrying Harley Davidson trips for two years.

Weird was the word for the first job. It sounded like an ideal company representative position dealing with other businesses. An advertising opportunity in me selling business stationery, pens, and other material. I was trained and apparently, I was given $200 in my bank account for expenses, and sample products and an order book. What happened was after approaching two or three businesses, who did not take up my offers, I was rather disappointed and did not do any more. That was interesting, as I never ever heard from the company who employed me, I'm not sure if I saw the $200, but I kept the pens. They must have forgotten about me.

The next, to me, was weirder. If not downright crazy. Centrelink sent me, as a senior person, to an agency in the Adelaide Hills that found work for over 60's. As I nominated experience in welding, they offered me a job on a cattle station off the Strzelecki track in the upper desert area of South Australia, as they needed a welder. I owned an early 90's Chrysler Valiant Station sedan which I had used in the private business. So, with Pauline's and the kids blessing I set off to the station. Now this car is low to the ground, and had suffered damage to the auto transmission sump, and exhaust, which had just been repaired.

The Strzelechi Track

This drive was an adventure, never having driven on the central area of the State, alone, to this remote area. The roads in the far north have reputations, especially the Strzelechi, so this I needed to tackle, thankfully in the spring. 520 kms after leaving Adelaide I arrived at Lyndhurst, a small outpost with a service station and a couple of buildings. I didn't take much notice apart from refuelling, so after that, I ventured to the end of the bitumen road, stopped, and thought, "This is it. 140 kms to go on this, yes, dirt road." Dirt road is an understatement, a boulder road is more to the point. This track is a challenge, so I drive off onto the dirt, and it wasn't long when the gravel started. There were paths where the gravel had been thrown to the side, but it was patchy. The noise of the gravel/stones on the 'track' was deafening. Two hours later I arrived at a small two-wheel track leading off to the left sign posted to the station I needed 25kms away. It was a pleasant drive on a sandy track to the place, almost as expected for an outback station of a large house and sheds. I managed to find a station hand who took me to the bunkhouse, where I dropped my gear, and went to the station house to meet the manager's wife. Before he left, he said, "A word of warning, be careful of the manager, we call him, 'The Storm,' he can be loud and aggressive, so treat him with caution. He is out and about now, so you will see him tomorrow."

After being fed, I met with the other station hands. The day temperature was moderate to high, and it was a full moon that night. The night temperature was cooler, so we all slept outside the shed. I was amazed at the brilliance of the night, with a perfectly clear sky where it was like daylight, I could read by the moonlight.

The next day, I met with the manager's son, Rob, and he took me around the shed areas, explaining that it was needed to build another cattle pen. Those of you who have seen movies and doco's about cattle ranches/stations will know what I mean. The pens consist of 2m high 3" steel pipe fences, all welded, strong enough to cope with huge wild cows and bulls at sale time. He then introduced me to the welding machine, pipe benders and structure. Well, I started work, and then broke the bending tool, that didn't help, and then struggled to use the antiquated welder and welding rod along with actually welding the pipe together. What a nightmare. I then realised I wasn't up to the job using tools I was unaccustomed to. In my struggles to do the job, Rob walked past a couple of times and never said a word. He must have seen I was stuffing up. Later in the day the Manager 'Storm' came to me and blasted me, accusing me of wasting material.

"Well, you are no good to me, you can get out of here, I need someone who can do the job properly." (interspersed with expletives.) Considering my history, this was a real test as I did not react, but I was humbled actually, and disappointed at not coming up to task. This man was really over the top and very aggressive. Supper time came and I was pleasantly surprised that all the hands, me included were fed at the master's table with a good spread of cooked food. Then came the nervous request from me to the boss as he offered the days wages: "Thank you. I'm sorry I couldn't do the job for you. But I ask if you could reimburse me for the drive up here, it cost me $200 to get here with fuel costs. I would appreciate it."

"If I must." He said angrily. I assured him I would leave in the morning. During the meal I realised that perhaps a reason for his aggressiveness, was firstly he was a very big overweight man with a stressed pain in his face. Then I saw that he was stuffing himself with food, and when he took up a slice of bread, he 'shovelled' a massive pile of butter on the bread and wolved it down. Fat, pure fat, Mr Stress was his name....

One more night sleeping in the moonlight on the dirt was a great experience but tainted with the previous day's events. Before I left, I spoke to Rob and explained to him that had he come to me to assist me in the job it might have been different, but I could not handle the size of the job through lack of experience and apologised to him. The drive out on that sandy track turned me into mush as I wept in prayer to my Lord realising perhaps this was a test for me in my dealings with aggressive people. This came about in another job as well.

The trip back to Adelaide was uneventful but also very tiring, as it amounted to over 1300kms in three days. As to that road, the noise of the large gravel was quite deafening, and on inspection, that transmission sump and exhaust needed fixing again. As few years later the grapevine informed me that the Station Manger died of a heart attack, I am not surprised.

Blue Plate Taxis

Another of these work attempts, was as a driver for a Company managing 'Blue Plate Taxis". They are in addition to the standard Taxi Companies, limousines hired by phone and not permitted to kerb hire. The vehicles were Ford Fairlane sedan cars. The company was not large, and had only fourteen vehicles, it was family owned but run by the son of the owner, I'll call him "Roger" as you will find out my reason soon. His father did the maintenance on the vehicles which happened occasionally. Fourteen-hour days appeared to be the norm, with very little work, and very little money to take home. Some of the jobs were good and lucrative, as he had the contract for the Veteran Affairs Govt Dept where I conveyed many returned soldiers to treatment centres and to and from the Daws Road Repatriation Hospital. It was a pleasure to look after these men with their PTSD problems, and to be part of their lives, as I often conveyed them several times.

As this job involved shifts, I needed to buy a motorcycle to get to and from the job in the city. So, I saw a Suzuki 650cc road bike with windscreen and panniers at a local bike shop which was the Japanese copy of the BSA 650 I rode in the police department those years ago, but this one had an electric starter motor, no kicking required. Pauline needed the car, so this purchase served two purposes, my desire to ride again, and for the work need.

This job almost tripped up my ego, as you may recall, I spent two years in the police operations room as a radio operator, apart from the work in the patrol cars with 'twenty-two years' experience in radio operation. Working for the young upstart in the office, 'Roger' I would attempt to correct his untrained radio procedures, which is really not the way to treat your boss. So, the term 'Roger, Roger' I believe I introduced. I did this as a matter of understanding what he was trying to say regarding the jobs and the call procedures.

This incident was almost comedic.... I mentioned the maintenance of the vehicles. On one hire I went to the West Beach Surf Life Saving Club, to an event where my passengers were the mayor of a city council and his wife to take home after the event. When I took possession of the vehicle at the start of my shift, I noticed that the rear air suspension was faulty to the point where there was no rear suspension at all. I was therefore totally embarrassed when my passengers were sitting in the rear seats feeling every bump. I did apologise to them. I was employed in the company for only eight months. At the start of any shift we, the drivers, were required to sign on and get the keys to our vehicles in a room to the rear of the operations room, which appeared to be becoming a fortress. It got worse to the point that we drivers were banned from any access to be able to do our job. The drivers could not even get access to get the car keys. I was at this time given a form of continued employment to complete, which I did. Roger then came out of his 'office' and spoke to me. I had been sitting there in the back room for some time and so I let him have it. I said angrily but with respect.

"Do you really expect me or any other driver to work under these conditions where we have no access to our keys or vehicles. Our wages are poor, you slug us $8 to do our paperwork among other charges, I work for fourteen hours and take home $2.50. You can keep your taxi business. I can no longer work here under these conditions." I walked out of there head high leaving Roger with nothing to say. A good test indeed, I finally felt able to cope with relationships with other people under stressful conditions, and to maintain decorum.

Harley Davidson Tours

My almost last short-term employment, which was not really employment, as mentioned in the first paragraph of this chapter, was professional motorcycle passenger hiring on a Harley Davidson, it was more a hobby. I have always dreamt of owning a Harley Davidson bike, as I owned an old 1926 machine as a teenager. It is rather vague as to how I came across this job, anyway, as I have had a history of motorcycle riding, and also as a member of the Ulysses Motorcycle Club, still owning the Suzuki GR650 road bike. Elek actually employed me to ride one of his Harley Davidson bikes. He was a one-man operation with contacts within other, perhaps, notorious clubs and individuals. He was a very sick man with Leukemia, although in recess, so he needed a rider to do his work.

I also believe that the Lord sent me to him to testify of His grace with the object of saving his soul. As it did not take long to realise, he was addicted to pornography and had a sexual appetite. So, I took opportunity to testify of God's grace. He accepted my testimonies but treated my witness with very light contempt. In saying that, he may not be alive now, so I do not know how his heart was with God.

I was involved in single person rides for up to four hours, and also group rides of up to ten individuals, some of whom were 'heavies' who tended to look at me sideways. I was not really liked by some of them, but I didn't care. Several country group rides occurred which were a real buzz, the main one was a New Year's Eve party at Port Vincent on Yorke Peninsular. There were five bikes, and we would take whoever on a lap of the entrance and exit roads of the town, about 5kms, for a fee. It was an exciting time.

The best ride I did, other than country rides with the Ulysses Club, was to take an intellectually challenged man, Mike, who was a Harley fan on a four-hour ride. I picked him up at his unit in Blackwood, and then I took the old original highway one to Murray Bridge which had absolutely no traffic on the very windy fast road, then the straight road to Wellington on the River Murray, where we had a minor breakdown. This was not surprising as on this trip I really let my hair down to experience the wind in the helmeted hair and in my glass covered eyes, at the fastest rate possible with care in my ability to handle this machine as taught professionally in the police department. What a whizz.....

The return trip back to Blackwood was via Strathalbyn, a very windy road. I only mention this for the sake of the immense experience, the breakdown, and then the final insult, I did not get paid for the ride. After we left Strathalbyn, it started raining. Now one does not ride on wet roads on a motorcycle unless unavoidable, so a slow ride on very windy roads, and then the downhill run on Upper Sturt Road. Well, this road had a high-profile curve over the road surface to the gutters, and it was wet. Being the careful rider I am, I needed to stop behind a car wanting to turn right, which I did by trying to keep on the top of the curve.

Oops, the bike slipped off to the left into the left kerb with my passenger still sitting on the pillion seat. I wish I had a camera for this one then. The one thing I learnt in motorcycle riding, if it falls over you must be able to pick it up. I did, I actually did, leaving Mike on the road, thankfully unhurt. The bike did have minor damage to the handlebars, so I did not earn a wage for that trip.

Now a Builder

Many years ago, in the early 80's while we were members of the Bethesda South Church, a Pastor prophesied over me with the words, "....The Lord has blessed the work of your hands......" This came to pass during the first decade of this century, in my move to work at the Youth With a Mission base at Norton Summit, as mentioned earlier. I was to work with the staff on work projects around the base for the next ten years on a part time basis, at two to three days per week. This was the start to the best part of our lives in working for the Lord in missionary work, over fifteen years.

This started when Pauline and I were drawn to YWAM, through an acquaintance where there was a call for volunteers to assist in various areas at the base. We attended a meeting with a large number of people, and I volunteered to assist in maintenance of the property, and Pauline with a Library. Enid, a lecturer at Tabor College met Pauline, and was the one who mentored her here to assist in working in a library at House of Prayer for All Nations at Aldgate, as Pauline was a qualified library technician. This was the start of a very new walk in the Christian church body for both of us, Pauline taking to the library situation like a duck to water. This era is spoken of in Chapter 19 in depth.

YWAM was also the place where my talents were upgraded with the assistance of the 'firms' regular carpenter as we worked together, and where I met Garry and Christie and his very young family. I really got on well with Garry and we became close friends, and as a result of his fitness regime I tried kept up to his physical fitness standard in regular running around the area with him. I must say it did help as I was overweight.

My biggest jobs there were roofing two 100,000 litre concrete rainwater tanks, also a large room extension involving the removal of one 500mm thick old stone wall of the original building to enlarge the dining room. This involved me put in a position of intermediary supervisor between the Mission Builders and Management.

My skills in building additions and alterations improved markedly in the building in of another verandah on the opposite side of the building with windows and constructing a large bench for the students on the base for computer operation. These two jobs became a very large project over three to four months. I also gained experience in the building of a large retaining wall using large sandstone blocks and a sunken rest area.

A different experience trained me for our Mission work overseas also mentioned in Chapter 9. Kris, the Manager of YWAM, permitted me to lecture to a group of students during a course held there, of my testimony as set out in this book. I was surprised at the reaction from them, as I saw a change in them accepting me as the grandfather of the base. It encouraged me when I saw tears from their eyes in one or two of them as they hugged me. I saw a generation gap broken. All glory to Him who saves.

My first job was that of building a timber frame around a rubbish disposal area, where posts were already in place. I did this in good faith with the materials at hand. Garry in his usual good humour checked it over, laughing as he said to me, "Graham, these beams are not straight..."

We really had a good laugh as he was right, and we then managed an understanding between us which eventually led to our invite to Russia after he moved to Krasnoyarsk with YWAM. He needed my building expertise which actually did improve as I explained above. When God leads, you follow.

The YWAM building experience saw me enrol at TAFE for obtaining a builder's licence to legally work as a builder. It was a huge experience going back to school, although when I first started running my garden waste removal business, I did a business course at TAFE which was very valuable. In that era also I enrolled in a private course for 'Occupational Health and Safety' which I did not complete due to other work commitments. All in years past.

Pauline's friend Enid lived in a house at Mt Barker in the Adelaide Hills. She had seen my work at YWAM and wanted to employ me to improve her home there. This was a huge challenge for me, so at the same time as I was doing the builder's licence course, I needed to be able to construct building plans on a computer. This experience was needed to do the job at her house. I was employed as an owner/builder for the job which avoided the necessity of having the builder's licence which I did not achieve as I could not finish the course due to the work required.

One of the adult students was a draftsman upgrading to the CAD program, and so I employed him to draw up plans for what Enid needed. This he did on instructions for the build, with one serious mistake. I am including this story to show that God is always in control. Enid was going to Indonesia to do a University curriculum and also to instruct students as a lecturer there in a Christian University. I was to do the main Job while she was there.

I was to remove some interior walls in the house to open the loungeroom to a larger area, replace the wall with LVL beams for ceiling support, and build a door into the ablution area entrance for separation, renew the bathroom, and repaint the area. Outside the house I was to build a 9 cubic metre extension attached to the house, remove an old double garage from the end of the driveway and replace with a new one, build a new fence between her driveway and the neighbour, install and plumb two 5000 litre rainwater tanks with a pump to use in the house; arrange for a plumber to install a new septic tank, and build a large above ground deck in the neck of the two right angle buildings which covered the new septic tank.

As you can see, it was another large project, this time, from the ground up similar to our own home which I built in Reynella years before. You may note that my skills were always being upgraded, job by job, in a very short time, acknowledging our Lord all the while. It took 1½ years to complete this job, at 2 to 3 days per week. I was also paid for this job, but at a minimum hourly rate to avoid having my Centrelink payments reduced. After finishing the internal renovation, I moved onto the planning for the extension. In the meantime, I removed the old garage and had the new one installed. Once Enid and I agreed on the design of the extension, I employed David, my draftsman, to draw the plans. This is the interesting part where I was not aware of his mistake until it came to build the walls, the building being brick veneer with brick and pier foundations up to 1-metre high for a timber floor. This was my problem now as I did not check the plans thoroughly. Now we know that God is in control.

I employed a brickie, John, for the foundation piers and the walls; he was loud, and a man of the world, who loved his beer. We had a good time together as I let him know my spiritual beliefs in general conversation, which he ignored, and we get into strong discussions around our differences. As a result, I was not aware for a while that he built the foundations one brick too high. He got so excited in our mutual conversations he lost concentration in planting too many bricks. I always have a chuckle over this mistake, but the atmosphere created an acceptable bond between us.

I then employed Ken and his son as carpenters to install the floor on the foundations. This carpenter was a genius, as we soon found the discrepancy in the height of the foundations. The plans were for 2.4m ceilings to fit against the back wall of the house for the roof on the extension to butt up to the rear wall of the house. But the one brick mistake put the roof too close to the house roof. So, we decided that if we increase the ceiling height to 3m, the roof lines would almost align. The difference along the length of the end of the house was only about 50mm, but the barge board at the front where the two roof angles met were perfectly aligned as it turned out. So now that the mistake in the plans showed that all roof angles on the majority of houses is 22.5 degrees, these plans had the roof angle at 22 degrees. My carpenter soon fixed this by raising the roof purlins to grade the level to match the old roof so that the angle was not noticeable.

Once the wall framing and roof timbers were complete, my brickie came back to build the walls, and we got on famously, becoming friends over the next year or so. I was also quite evangelical with my carpenter with the same results and we also became friends over the next few years where I was always welcome in his home, as with my brickie. This was God's grace in action where I have no idea what effect our relationships would have had on them with my testimony.

The detail here listed, shows where plans and mistakes were made in the build but to me, God's inspiration changed the mistakes to that of the greater good in providing Enid with a better home, by His direction and blessing in using my hands in the effort and joy of doing the job. When I had finished the work required, Enid was very happy with the results and leased the house to a young family known to her, so when Enid's tenure was completed in Indonesia, she sold the house after the young family moved to Perth and claimed a 1/3rd increase in the house value as a result of the renovations.

I went into this job in my senior years, an amateur, and came out close to being professional, while completing minor jobs in the southern area where I lived by word of mouth. But I declined doing this by not having achieved my builder's licence, and I was also getting too long in the tooth to do the jobs accurately and quickly.

So, God certainly did bless the work of my hands quite successfully over a ten-year period, covering post retirement to our efforts in overseas ministry from 2012 to 2018.

20

Another Trial

This chapter amplifies the incidents mentioned in earlier chapters. Our family were members of a church fellowship in the Southern area of Adelaide, a branch of the Bethesda group, where we grew spiritually over a period of 33 years. God used us in many ways, our 3 children being musicians in this church for a number of those years. Pauline was part of a bible college as librarian at this fellowship, and I had been trained in prayer ministry, albeit briefly, but with divine results. Throughout this period, we submitted to 3 pastoral ministries, Dean, who I have already mentioned earlier, brought me through my internment, and then he was transferred to a ministry on the Yorke Peninsular, having grown in his faith and abilities from a Deacon. He was replaced by a senior pastor and apostle Tim Jack, who led the church into a higher level of faith and prayer. A great mentor and leader.

Tim then appointed a young couple to replace him, to lead the church as he was transferred to Geelong as head of the Apostolic Network. During this time, under the new leadership some years later, I was having trouble with this leader with his music, which was not to my liking and I did not believe the style was worshipful. I had spoken to him about this but did not get any satisfaction. Unfortunately, as I considered the music style to be rather of the world, I had to walk out during services to get some peace, as I could not worship the Lord. It happened once too often, and my emotions let go. As a result, I was counselled by my study pastor and the pastor, who must remain un-named.

Pauline and I were so upset by this situation, we were forced to leave the fellowship. This was quite traumatic for both of us, as we had been there for 33 years and had to pull away from friends in the fellowship until it all settled down. So, we went away to the Flinders ranges for a few days where we laid our lives at the Lord's feet. We shed many tears at this stage in our lives as we sought His guidance scripturally. We just sat in our car at a small car park just off the road and looked out over the beautiful scenery in front of us, and with tears we read scripture, which indicated a path given and felt by our Lord. Unfortunately, we did not make notes of the verses. We felt the peace as we sat there, but also a deep sadness. It was decided then that we would join Ps Jenny's group of intercessors where Pauline was working in her resource centre.

The New Path

This new path was already set by the Holy Spirit. As mentioned earlier, Pauline was now involved in her own library at AHOP at Aldgate, so we then found that Jenny Hagger had fellowship meetings at Hahndorf with her intercessory group of believers. We had a new place to worship God and meet many more of His saints.

This fellowship met in a large building at the Hahndorf Motel on a weekly basis, where large gatherings of people assembled when invited speakers would minister. The teachings and fellowship were outstanding and totally different to what we were accustomed. The Holy Spirit's presence was quite strong where our eyes were opened even further to the giftings and bible teaching. Suddenly we were involved with 24/7 prayer and intersession, and spiritual warfare.

To me this was a third level of experience, distinct from the formal non-charismatic fellowship to the Pentecostal movement, and then the prayer movement. My wife and I have now been with this fellowship, for 11 years.

Due to experience with media in operating a video camera and the processing of DVDs at our earlier Church, I took on the role of media person for the group for several years, working with others, until my attention span was dropping. My professional assistant David took the reins, along with Pastor Mario.

Pauline and I have seen a total transformation in our lives spiritually since worshipping with AHOP under Apostle Jenny's leadership. Her husband, Pastor Brian, I must say has a habit during worship services, of testing one's faith, by tapping someone on the shoulder, asking, "Would you please share around the Communion table this morning." A little apprehension surfaced here.

I always have nodded in the positive when he has asked me by this means. In doing so the Holy Spirit has always responded by giving a message of inspiration which is fitting for the occasion. In fact, several times, I have been given a scripture and message to share before leaving home with that small voice saying, "Brian will ask you this morning." Even while in the meeting, the Holy Spirit has said, "Brian will call on you this morning." Then gives me the word to share. The interesting part of this Pentecostal fellowship is that the system used extensively in the Pentecostal church is the use of the spiritual gifts in tongues and interpretation according to the Corinthian letters of the apostle Paul. These gifts being for the edification of the body and the individual.

This is actually rare, but done differently, being a small group of mature people. The Holy Spirit edifies towards the issues of the time with scripture, and prophetic words in English. I could say with confidence that this usually occurs. At times, when I have shared around the communion table, the words given to me have been so powerful that I have actually fallen to the floor weeping with the release. On rare occasions the same has happened when I have given a prophetic word.

Here I give Pauline much credit for her work in the library at the offices at Aldgate, as she is held in high regard by Jenny and her team for the effort she has put into same. The library is a resource centre for the body of Christ having been built up over these 11 years to over 10,000 books. Now both of us being over 75 years of age, we continue to be part of a vibrant fellowship of beautiful people where love is the binding of this body. To God's Glory.

About the Author

In Chapter 2, I set out my family legacy regarding my parents and my life so I may be repeating some aspect of my story. Most of my life I have always wondered how my parents met. I never thought to ask them or their families, so I have remained in ignorance. The only clue is that Clem was a footballer of some repute in Penola in the south east and was selected to play for the Sturt football Club in Adelaide, but due to a stomach ulcer, (which probably made him the grumpy old sod that he was), he was not afforded the opportunity of playing football for Sturt, or enlist for war service for that matter, hence being employed at the Holdens motor vehicle factory at Woodville.

One can only assume that tensions were there between my parents, as my father relented and as a family, we moved from their first home together at Croydon to Aldgate Valley only 5km's from Mylor, so mother could be closer to her family. I was born at North Adelaide and my first home being at the Croydon bungalow. My parents bought a property of 10 acres at Aldgate, employing a cow which we milked, chickens which gave us eggs, and a shotgun for the brown snakes. It was called 'The Pines' on the Valley Road. My father then needed to commute from Aldgate to Woodville by train, being away from home 6am to 6pm, which may have caused some tension, which would affect their relationship. It would have for me.

I can only assume also, that their attitudes had an emotional effect on me which was a driver to some of my attitudes and introversion. As my life has gone on, I realise I am no different to any other person on the planet, but every person lives a different life, so an understanding of this gives an appreciation that we treat each other with respect and dignity as we expect to be treated. It's called, I believe, compassion and empathy. This during my time in the police department, this was not the case, I was a persecutor. What can I say about my change of character, a renewed spirit to compassion and empathy? Only a commitment to Jesus Christ and His word is the way, truth and life. John 3.16.

The one major consideration is, from this testimony, it is obvious that regardless of my change from sinner to saint, is that I was not completely changed, I still had choices. As a 'Christian', I was still not capable of making all of the right choices, I failed in several areas where extreme measures were necessary to get me on the right path. My major mistakes were as a Christian, not as a person of the world. Hypocrisy the order of the day.

By reading back through this testimonial, I still find it difficult in understanding myself, and my actions throughout my life, when it occurred to me, that even with a renewed Spirit as a born-again spirit filled follower of Jesus Christ, that as this testimonial amplifies is the huge mistakes in managing my emotions and abilities to make emotional decisions. I failed and committed massive crimes delivering pain to others, bringing about internment penalties to bring me into line.

We need to understand we are fighting a spiritual battle, between good and evil where the power of that opposition is greater than ours, so our need to be closer to God, and His Word, and especially with the gift of the power and authority of that Holy Spirit in our lives, in my life now, that my weaknesses need to be overcome by that authority.

I could quote many Scriptures to back my statements, but I leave that to you to search for them, as this is an autobiography, not a Bible Study. My life now with my dear Pauline, has settled into old age routine, but with our Christian Community there where we soak up the love of the Body of Christ, with our Apostle Jenny and team whom we support.

The story is not over yet, the drama continues. I have been a slow learner, and like every person we have our lives to lead, along with whatever is placed in front of us, the difficulty is, by whose strength do we go to for helping us to overcome our personal drama's.

This book of my life is designed to explain what happened to me in order to survive, not by myself, as this was not possible. It took God's hand on my shoulder to push me in the right direction not as a robot but by my ability or inability to make the right decisions. God has a plan for all humanity, it is our choice to make the right decisions according to His guidance. He is perfect love, His son Jesus is His love personified, His Holy Spirit is our helper, and available to anoint us with power and authority for His purposes in our lives. I put forward a challenge to all who read this, to take hold of that perfect love where Jesus sacrificed His body for our healing and spill His blood for our redemption, so we have Eternal Life in Him.

Revelation 1:8, "I am the Alpha and the Omega," declares the Lord God, "the one who is, who was, and who is coming, the Almighty."

Revelation 2:7 ".....To everyone who conquers I will give the privilege of eating from the tree of life that is in God's Paradise.

We now await His return and any leading into sharing the Gospel in our Community.

Amen.

www.ingramcontent.com/pod-product-compliance
Lightning Source LLC
Chambersburg PA
CBHW030254010526
44107CB00053B/1711